Scotland's leading educational publishers

CW01263666

National 4 & 5
HEALTH & FOOD TECHNOLOGY
COURSE NOTES

N4 & 5 HEALTH & FOOD TECHNOLOGY *COURSE NOTES*

Edna Hepburn • Lynn Smith

© 2013 Leckie & Leckie Ltd
Cover image © K. Miri Photography

001/03062013

10 9 8 7 6 5 4

ISBN 9780007504763

Published by
Leckie & Leckie Ltd
An imprint of HarperCollins*Publishers*
Westerhill Road, Bishopbriggs, Glasgow, G64 2QT
T: 0844 576 8126   F: 0844 576 8131
leckieandleckie@harpercollins.co.uk
www.leckieandleckie.co.uk

Special thanks to
Helen Bleck (copy-edit); Jouve (layout); Ink Tank (cover design); Anna Penman (proofread); Jill Laidlaw (proofread)

Printed and bound by CPI Group (UK) Ltd, Croydon, CR0 4YY

A CIP Catalogue record for this book is available from the British Library.

Acknowledgements
We would like to thank the following for permission to reproduce photographs. Page numbers are followed, where necessary, by t (top), b (bottom), m (middle), l (left) or r (right).

P6–7 Subbotina Anna, p9l Elena Schweitzer, p9r iStockphoto, p10l Gyuszko-Photo, p10r Evgenia Sh, p10b YanLev, p12l Joshua Resnick, p12r Sandra Caldwell, p14t Gl0ck, p14r Brent Hofacker, p15t Maria Komar, p15m bergamont, p15b Jiri Hera, p17t Nathan B Dappen, p17b Squareplum, p18t Maen CG, p18b Elenamiv, p19t Elena Schweitzer, p19b Pavels Rumme, p20 monticello, p21t Lightspring, p21b Alex Mit, p22 Dionisvera, p23t Keith Wilson, p24 Nitr, p25t Jaimie Duplass, p25b Imageman, p26 Cathleen A Clapper, p27 Robyn Mackenzie, p28b Robyn Mackenzie, p29t Razmarinka, p29b foodonwhite, p30 Aaron Amat, p31 Tish1, p32 tacar, p34 Lilyana Vynogradova, p37tl Tischenko Irina, p37tr Monticello, p37bl Oliver Hoffmann, p37br Robyn Mackenzie, p38 Scisetti Alfio, p41tl Juriah Mosin, p41tm Alexey Stiop, p41tr Lisa F. Young, p41tm Serenethos, p41rb Diedie, p41bm samoshkin, p41lm SeanPavonePhoto, p46 Whiterabbit83, p48l Goodluz, p48r Peter Bernik, p52 Joe Gough, p53t iStockphoto, p53m Rafal Olechowski, p53b iStockphoto, p54 Anatoliy Samara, p55 iStockphoto, p56t Monkey Business Images, p56b Indigo Fish, p57 iStockphoto, p58 Martin Novak, p59 Lilyana Vynogradova, p61 ariadna de raadt, p64 Monkey Business Images, p65 Africa Studio, p68 iStockphoto, p69 iStockphoto, p70t iStockphoto, p71 Leelaryonkul, p73 Dmitry Lobanov, p74t Brent Hofacker, p74b Alila Medical Images, p75 Potapov Alexander, p78t iStockphoto, p78b Picsfive, p79bl Eskemar, P86–87 luchschen, p88 Olinchuk, p89t bitt24, p89m abimages, p89b Evikka, p90t Warren Price Photography, p90b Mike Flippo, p91 bergamont, p93tl ffolas, p93tr Crepesoles, p93bl iStockphoto, p93 Marie C Fields, p94 Michal Modzelewski, p96m Anna Sedneva, p106 Benjamin Brosdau, p108t Fusebulb, p108b Sebastian Kaulitzki, p110t Kharkhan Oleg, p110b iStockphoto, p114 Lim Yong Hian, p120 jannoon028, p121 iStockphoto, p123 Food & Drug Administration/Science Photo Library, p124 iStockphoto, p135t koya979, p135b Thomas Northcut, p136t Joe Gough/Nayashkova Olga, p136b istockphoto, p137t Brian A Jackson, p137b travellight, p144 koko-tewan, p145t Peter Bernik, p145b iStockphoto, p146 iStockphoto, p149t Franck Boston/Stephen Finn, p149b iStockphoto, p151t Evgeny Karandaev, p151tm Berents, p151bm Sergio Stakhnyk, p151b Betacam-SP, p160tl Joe Gough, p160tr Brian A Jackson, p160bl iStockphoto, p161tl Timmary, p161tr pedrosala, p169 Bernabea Amalia Mendez, p180 Smit, p183t Brian A Jackson, p183b iStockphoto, p185m Brian A Jackson, p186 STILLFX, p201 Brent Hofacker

We would like to thank the following organisations for permission to reproduce logos.

P79 Coaliac UK, p147 Soil Association, p154 Fairtrade, p165 Benecol, p167 Quorn™, p176 Trading Standards Institute, p177 Which? (The copyright in this material is owned by Which? Limited and has been reproduced here with their permission. The material and logo must not be reproduced in whole or in part without the written permission of Which? Limited.) p186 Vegetarian Society

Whilst every effort has been made to trace the copyright holders, in cases where this has been unsuccessful, or if any have inadvertently been overlooked, the Publishers would gladly receive any information enabling them to rectify any error or omission at the first opportunity.

Contents

CONTENTS

Answers to *Test your knowledge* questions are available to download, free, from the Leckie & Leckie website. Go to www.leckieandleckie.co.uk/n45health

Introduction

What's this book about?

The chapters in this book cover the three units you have to complete to achieve the National 4 and 5 Health & Food Technology courses.

The three units are:

1. Food for Health
2. Food Product Development
3. Contemporary Food Issues

At the start of each unit there is:

- a short description of the unit

- the two outcomes (what you have to do)

- what you have to know or do to pass each outcome of the unit (i.e. the Assessment Standards).

How are the units assessed?

Each of the Outcomes and Assessment Standards in the units have to be assessed.

This can be done in three ways:

1. Unit by unit assessment – this means that each unit is assessed separately.
2. Portfolio of assessments – this means that each assessment standard is assessed separately.
3. Combined assessment – this means that either two units or three units can be combined and assessed together.

Course Assessment

There are two parts to the National 5 course assessment:

- An assignment worth 50 marks. The assignment has four sections:
  - Section 1: Planning
  - Section 2: The product
  - Section 3: Product testing
  - Section 4: Evaluation

> ⚠ **Watch point**
> It is important to keep all assessment evidence together and to ensure that all of your work is dated.

- A question paper worth 50 marks. Marks are allocated approximately as follows:
  - 20 marks will be based on Food for Health
  - 10 marks will be based on Food Product Development
  - 20 marks will be based on Contemporary Food Issues

At National 4 the course assessment is an assignment to produce a food product for a given brief.

UNIT 1: FOOD FOR HEALTH.

This unit will develop your knowledge and understanding of the link between food, nutrition and health. You will look at the importance of having a balanced diet and various ways of achieving this through following current dietary advice.

You will develop an understanding of the dietary needs of groups of people and the effect of diet-related conditions on their health.

Practical activities will allow you to produce food products linked to each of the topics you are studying.

This unit will also give you the opportunity to work through some of the types of questions you might meet in the course assessment question paper.

By the end of this unit you should be able to:

OUTCOME 1: EXPLAIN THE RELATIONSHIP BETWEEN HEALTH, FOOD, AND NUTRITION.

This means you have to:

- Describe the benefits to health of a balanced and varied diet.
- Describe, in detail, current dietary advice.
- Explain the function and effects on health of the main nutrients.
- Explain the effects of diet-related conditions or diseases on health.

OUTCOME 2: MAKE AND REFLECT ON A FOOD PRODUCT TO MEET DIETARY AND HEALTH NEEDS.

This means you have to:

- Explain the dietary and health needs of a specified individual or group of individuals.
- Select and use appropriate ingredients and cooking methods to make a food product to meet the dietary and health needs of a specified individual or group of individuals.
- Explain how the food product meets the dietary and health needs of a specified individual or group of individuals.

1
Food for Health

1 Functions and effects on health of the main nutrients, water and dietary fibre

After completing this chapter you should be able to:

- Explain the function and effects on health of the macro-nutrients: protein, fats and carbohydrates.
- Explain the function and effects on health of micro-nutrients: vitamins and minerals.
- Explain the function and effects on health of water and dietary fibre.
- Explain the inter-relationship of nutrients.
- Describe the effects of storage, preparation and cooking on nutrients.

The above statements are called objectives.

Make the link

Throughout this chapter refer to further information about nutrients linked to individual needs in Chapter 3.

Topic 1: Nutrients

Nutrients are substances contained in food that are essential to keep us alive and healthy and are grouped into macro- and micro-nutrients.

What are macro-nutrients?

Macro-nutrients are the main nutrients needed by the body in relatively large amounts. They include protein, fats and carbohydrates.

Proteins: why do we need them?

The **main functions** of protein in the body are:

- growth and repair of body cells
- maintenance of body cells.

The **secondary** function of protein in the body is:

- to provide energy.

Proteins: what are they and where do we get them?

Proteins are **vital** to life. They are made up of building blocks known as **amino acids**, some of which are **essential**.

Where a protein contains **all** the essential amino acids, they are known as High Biological Value (HBV) proteins. Mainly animal sources.

Where a protein **lacks one or more** of the essential amino acids, they are known as Low Biological Value (LBV) proteins. Mainly vegetable sources.

High Biological Value proteins are found in:

- meat
- fish
- cheese
- milk
- eggs.

HBV protein is also found in soya beans, an essential source for vegetarians.

Low Biological Value proteins are found in:

- cereals, e.g. wheat, rice, oats
- pulses, e.g. peas, beans, lentils
- some nuts.

LBV protein is also found in gelatine (animal source).

It is important to include a variety of LBV proteins in your diet to ensure you get all the essential amino acids, e.g. lentil soup with wholemeal bread; three-bean chilli with rice.

The effect on health if the protein balance is not right

Not enough	Too much
Growth in children is slowed down	Can be converted to fat in the body and can lead to obesity if it is not used up as a secondary source of energy
Cuts and wounds will take longer to heal	

Protein deficiency is rare in the UK, however in poor countries it can lead to conditions such as retarded growth, chronic infections, poor quality hair and skin conditions.

Proteins – know the facts

HBV proteins are the best source of protein and are mainly of animal origin.

A number of new products are being developed to supply HBV protein for the growing number of vegetarians. These include foods like Quorn™, tofu, soya milk and products, and vegetarian cheeses.

Let's Cook

Time to make a dish which includes protein.

Examples of HBV dishes you could make (substitute the meat with Quorn™ for vegetarians):

1. Spaghetti bolognese
2. Chilli con carne
3. Lasagne

✔ Test your knowledge

1. What are 'macro-nutrients'?
2. Give two functions of protein in the diet.
3. What do the abbreviations HBV and LBV stand for?
4. Describe the difference between HBV and LBV proteins and give two examples of each.
5. Explain one effect on health of having too much protein in the diet.

Answers to all **Test your knowledge** questions can be downloaded from www.leckieandleckie. co.uk/n45health

Carbohydrates: what are they and where do we get them?

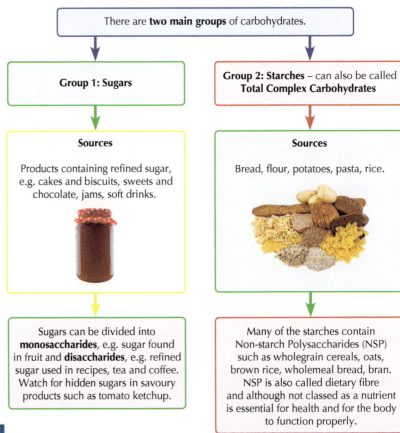

There are **two main groups** of carbohydrates.

Group 1: Sugars

Group 2: Starches – can also be called **Total Complex Carbohydrates**

Sources

Products containing refined sugar, e.g. cakes and biscuits, sweets and chocolate, jams, soft drinks.

Sources

Bread, flour, potatoes, pasta, rice.

Sugars can be divided into **monosaccharides**, e.g. sugar found in fruit and **disaccharides**, e.g. refined sugar used in recipes, tea and coffee. Watch for hidden sugars in savoury products such as tomato ketchup.

Many of the starches contain Non-starch Polysaccharides (NSP) such as wholegrain cereals, oats, brown rice, wholemeal bread, bran. NSP is also called dietary fibre and although not classed as a nutrient is essential for health and for the body to function properly.

Carbohydrates: why do we need them?

The **main functions** of carbohydrates in the body are:

- to supply energy for all activities
- to supply warmth and so help maintain normal body temperature.

The effect on health if the carbohydrate balance is not right

Not enough	Too much
A lack of energy leading to tiredness	Can be converted to fat in the body and can lead to obesity
Protein may be used as a source for energy instead of growth and repair	Too much sugar can lead to dental caries or diabetes

Complex carbohydrates – know the facts

It is recommended that we get most of our energy from starch or Total Complex Carbohydrates (TCC) for the following reasons:

1. Starches are good sources of other nutrients, e.g. potatoes are a good source of vitamin C; bread supplies protein, calcium and iron.

2. They bulk out the diet and make you feel fuller for longer.

3. They do not encourage dental caries – bacteria in the mouth do not like starches.

Sugar – know the facts

Sugar is often referred to as an 'empty calorie' food as it provides energy and no other nutritional value.

Sugar can be classified as:

*   Intrinsic sugars: these are naturally occurring sugars in food, e.g. fruit and vegetables.

*   Extrinsic sugars: these are sugars added to foods, e.g. refined sugar, extracted sugar in honey. They are known as Non-Milk Extrinsic Sugar (NMES).

✔ Test your knowledge

1. What are the two groups of carbohydrates?
2. What do the abbreviations NSP and TCC stand for?
3. Which type of carbohydrate – sugars or starches – is the better one to eat? Give two reasons why.
4. Explain the difference between intrinsic and extrinsic sugars.
5. Describe two functions of carbohydrates in the diet.

Let's Cook

Time to make a dish which includes carbohydrates.

Examples of dishes you could make:

1. Pizza/bruschetta
2. Tomato and basil pasta
3. Individual sponge cakes/ lemon drizzle cakes

Fats: what are they and where do we get them?

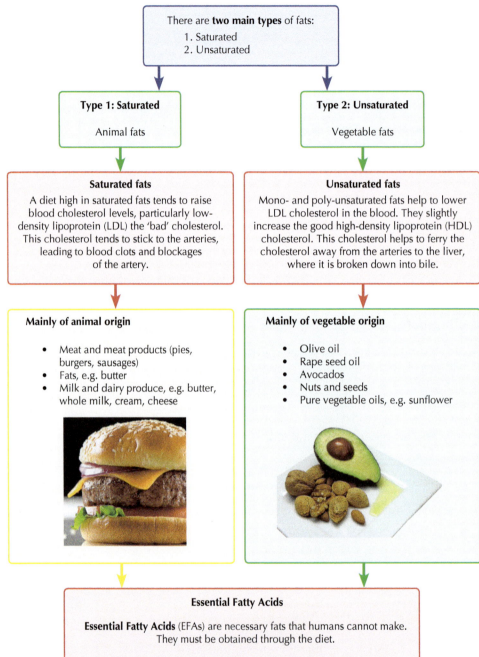

There are **two main types** of fats:
1. Saturated
2. Unsaturated

Type 1: Saturated

Animal fats

Type 2: Unsaturated

Vegetable fats

Saturated fats

A diet high in saturated fats tends to raise blood cholesterol levels, particularly low-density lipoprotein (LDL) the 'bad' cholesterol. This cholesterol tends to stick to the arteries, leading to blood clots and blockages of the artery.

Unsaturated fats

Mono- and poly-unsaturated fats help to lower LDL cholesterol in the blood. They slightly increase the good high-density lipoprotein (HDL) cholesterol. This cholesterol helps to ferry the cholesterol away from the arteries to the liver, where it is broken down into bile.

Mainly of animal origin

- Meat and meat products (pies, burgers, sausages)
- Fats, e.g. butter
- Milk and dairy produce, e.g. butter, whole milk, cream, cheese

Mainly of vegetable origin

- Olive oil
- Rape seed oil
- Avocados
- Nuts and seeds
- Pure vegetable oils, e.g. sunflower

Essential Fatty Acids

Essential Fatty Acids (EFAs) are necessary fats that humans cannot make. They must be obtained through the diet.

The main EFA is omega-3 – it helps to reduce the risk of blood clots, heart attacks and rheumatoid arthritis.

Omega-3 is needed for brain development in babies and young children.

Fat: why do we need it?

The **main functions** of fat in the body are:

- To provide warmth through an insulated layer under the skin.

- To provide a concentrated source of energy.

- To provide the fat-soluble vitamins A, D, E and K.

- To provide essential fatty acids.

- To surround and protect the vital organs such as the kidneys.

The effect on health if the fat balance is not right

Not enough	Too much
The intake of essential fatty acids such as Omega-3 may be reduced	Can lead to obesity
Fat soluble vitamins may be reduced	Can lead to high blood pressure and coronary heart disease

Fats – know the facts

There are 'visible' and 'invisible' fats.

Visible fat is easy to see – fat on meat, and in butter, margarine, cooking oil.

Invisible fat is a constituent part of the food and is difficult to detect – fat in cakes, biscuits, pastry.

The term fat includes both 'fats' and 'oils'.

Fats are solid at room temperature and are the saturated fats, e.g. butter.

Oils are liquid at room temperature and are the unsaturated fats, e.g. cooking oil.

Beware of the trans-fatty acid

Trans-fatty acids, or hydrogenated fats as they are sometimes known, are polyunsaturated fats which have been artificially hardened by adding extra hydrogen. These cause an increased risk of heart disease, rheumatoid arthritis and are linked to some cancers. They are found in hard margarine, biscuits, cakes, commercially fried foods, e.g. french fries from fast-food outlets. Beware of foods that have hydrogenated fats on the label.

Let's Cook

Time to make a dish which reduces fat in the diet.

Examples of dishes you could make:

1. Stir-fry
2. Tuna pasta bake with low-fat cheese and semi-skimmed milk
3. Mackerel and pasta salad

Test your knowledge

1. What are the two types of fat?
2. Explain two functions of fats in the diet.
3. What do the abbreviations LDL and HDL cholesterol stand for and what is the difference between the two types of cholesterol?
4. What are trans-fatty acids? Explain their effect on health.
5. What are essential fatty acids and why should we include them in diet?

The effects of storage, preparation and cooking on macro-nutrients

Storage

Nutrient	Effect on macro-nutrient
Fats	Exposure to air leads to deterioration and rancidity of fats. To prevent this, store in the fridge and out of direct light. • Fats become rancid due to **oxidation** – oxygen is absorbed by the fat molecules and reacts to produce an unpleasant flavour and colour. • **Oxidation** is accelerated by light and any impurities in the fat.

Preparation

Nutrient	Effect on macro-nutrient
Fats	• A concentration of fat makes it more difficult to digest. It becomes easier to digest when the surface of the food is broken down before exposing it to the digestive system, e.g. grated cheese. • Combining a starchy food, e.g. cheese, with potatoes or macaroni will help absorb the fat, making it easier to digest.

Cooking

Nutrient	Effect on macro-nutrient
Protein	• Protein coagulates or sets when heated, e.g. egg white sets. • Heating the protein in wheat (gluten) helps bread to hold its structure. • Protein in milk forms a skin on the surface when heated. • Protein in meat shrinks when heated. • Overheating makes protein less easy to digest.
Fats	• Solid fats melt to liquid on heating. • Fats are fairly stable to heat at normal cooking temperatures. However, if oil continues to be heated a blue haze will be given off and the fat will ignite. • When a fat reaches smoking point it will go rancid and smell.
Carbohydrates	
Starch	**Effects of dry heat – dextrinisation** • Dextrin is formed when foods containing starch are subject to dry heat, e.g. toasting bread. • Dextrinisation gives baked items a brown colour. • Overheating of starch causes charring and burning. **Effects of moist heat on starch/solubility** • When a moist heat is applied to starch the starch grains soften and swell. They then absorb moisture, which causes the grains to rupture. When this happens, starch is released and forms a gel, e.g. when white sauce is thickened.
Sugar	**Effects of heat on sugar – caramelisation** 1. Dry heat • Sugar melts then caramelises, going brown and then burning. • The caramelisation of the sugar forms a golden crust on baked items. 2. Moist heat • Sugar dissolves and with prolonged heating at high temperatures it becomes a syrup, which caramelises then chars when the water has evaporated.

Make the link

Look at the chapter on food product development for further information.

Let's Cook

Time to make a dish which shows the effects of preparation, storage and cooking on macro-nutrients.

Examples of dishes you could make:

1. Macaroni cheese
2. Crème brûlée/crème caramel
3. Bread (bread mix)

Test your knowledge

1. Describe how fat may become rancid during storage.
2. Give two examples showing the coagulation of protein in cooking.
3. State the changes that take place when a solid fat is:
   i. Heated
   ii. Overheated.
4. Identify the type of protein found in wheat which helps to hold the structure.
5. Explain the term 'dextrinisation'.
6. Cheese, due to the fat content, is sometimes difficult to digest.
   State two ways during food preparation that cheese could be made easier to digest.

Topic 2: Micro-nutrients: vitamins

Micro-nutrients: what are they?

Micro-nutrients are the nutrients needed by the body in smaller amounts. They include vitamins and minerals.

Vitamins: what are they and where do we get them?

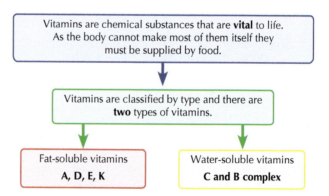

Vitamins are chemical substances that are **vital** to life. As the body cannot make most of them itself they must be supplied by food.

Vitamins are classified by type and there are **two** types of vitamins.

Fat-soluble vitamins
A, D, E, K

Water-soluble vitamins
C and B complex

Fat-soluble vitamins

Vitamin A

Functions: why do we need vitamin A?

1. To make visual purple, a substance in the eye, to assist in good vision, particularly in dim light.

2. To keep the mucous membranes healthy.

3. For the maintenance of healthy skin.

4. For normal growth in children.

Vitamin A is an antioxidant vitamin (see page 23 for further information).

Sources: where can we find vitamin A?

It can be found in both animal and plant sources.

Animal sources	Plant sources
Milk	Carrots
Cheese	Tomatoes
Eggs	Apricots
Oily fish	Spinach
Liver	Cabbage

The effect on health if vitamin A balance is not right

Not enough	Too much
Reduced vision in dim light leading to night blindness	During pregnancy too much vitamin A can be harmful to the developing foetus. However, it is important to get the balance right to prevent pregnant women becoming vitamin A deficient.
Dry and infected skin and mucous membranes	

⚠ Watch point

Vitamin supplements can be harmful if too many are taken; it is better to get the right balance of vitamins from the diet.

🔍 Hint

Vitamin A is added to margarine by law (this is called fortification).

⚠ Watch point

A lack of vitamin A can cause poor growth in children, especially in developing countries.

☑ Test your knowledge

1. Explain two functions of vitamin A.

2. Describe two effects on health caused by a deficiency of vitamin A.

3. Name two plant and two animal sources of vitamin A.

🍴 Let's Cook

Time to make a dish which includes vitamin A.

Examples of dishes you could make:

1. Sweet potato and red pepper soup

2. Mediterranean couscous

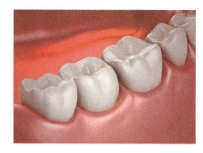

Vitamin D

Functions: why do we need vitamin D?

1. For the proper formation of bones and teeth.

2. To promote quicker healing of bone fractures.

3. Required for the absorption of calcium and phosphorus.

Sources: where can we find vitamin D?

This is the **sunshine** vitamin, as the main source is the sun's ultra violet rays. A substance under the skin is converted to vitamin D and the sun can supply all the body's required vitamin D.

Food sources

- Cod liver oil
- Oily fish
- Liver
- Egg yolk
- Fortified foods such as margarine and breakfast cereals

The effect on health if vitamin D balance is not right

Not enough	Too much
Poor growth and a risk of rickets in children where bones become soft and bend	Very rare but can lead to deposits of calcium in the blood and heart
Osteomalacia (adult rickets) in the elderly	
People at risk of vitamin D deficiency include those who are housebound, or whose religion requires them to wear covering clothes such as burkas or trousers and long-sleeved tops and hats	

Let's Cook

Time to make a dish which includes vitamin D.

Examples of dishes you could make:

1. Tuna pizza
2. Mackerel paté

☑ Test your knowledge

1. Describe two functions of vitamin D in the diet.
2. Give effects on health of vitamin D deficiency.
3. Apart from the diet, state one other source of vitamin D.

Vitamin E

Functions: why do we need vitamin E?

1. To help prevent certain cancers and heart disease.

2. For healthy skin.

Vitamin E is a very effective antioxidant vitamin (see page 23 for further information).

Sources: Where can we find vitamin E?

- Eggs
- Nuts
- Seeds
- Cereal products
- Vegetable oil

Deficiencies: what will happen if I don't get enough vitamin E?

Deficiency of vitamin E is very rare. However, premature babies may be placed in a special baby care unit where they can receive vitamin E to reduce or prevent damage to their eyes.

> ⚠️ **Watch point**
>
> - According to some studies, vitamin E slows down the ageing process.
> - Researchers believe that vitamin E plays a role in the prevention of cancers and heart disease.
> - Cut down on deep-frying foods as this method of cookery destroys vitamin E.

☑️ Test your knowledge

1. What is the importance of vitamin E in the diet?
2. Why do premature babies receive vitamin E?
3. Which method of cooking destroys vitamin E?

> **Let's Cook**
>
> Time to make a dish which includes vitamin E.
>
> Examples of dishes you could make:
>
> 1. Broccoli pasta bake
> 2. Mango salsa

Vitamin K

Functions: why do we need vitamin K?

- Vitamin K is important for ensuring that the blood clots when injured, so preventing harmful blood loss.

Sources: where can we find vitamin K?

- Green vegetables
- Pulses
- Fruits
- Cereals
- Meat and liver

> 🔍 **Hint**
>
> Bacteria that are usually present in the intestines also produce a useful supply of vitamin K.

Deficiencies: what will happen if I don't get enough vitamin K?
Blood may not clot properly, increasing the possibility of harmful blood loss after an injury.

A deficiency is rare but all babies are given a vitamin K injection immediately after they are born to ensure their blood will clot if they are injured.

Let's Cook

Time to make a dish which includes vitamin K.

Examples of dishes you could make:

1. Spicy noodles with spinach, broccoli and sugar snap peas
2. Apple and plum crumble

☑ Test your knowledge

1. Why do babies receive a vitamin K injection?
2. Give two examples of foods containing vitamin K.
3. Describe the function of vitamin K in the diet.

Water-soluble vitamins

Consuming large quantities of water soluble vitamins does not usually have any bad effect on our health. We should eat foods containing water soluble vitamins every day, as our bodies do not store them in the same way as fat soluble vitamins.

Vitamin B complex

There are many types of vitamin B, so this group is often called 'vitamin B complex'.

Why do we need each of the vitamin B complex and where do they come from?

Vitamin B1 (thiamine)	Vitamin B2 (riboflavin)	Vitamin B3 (niacin)

Functions: why is vitamin B complex needed for health?
- Helps release energy from carbohydrates
- For growth and normal function of the nervous system
- For normal growth in children

Sources: where can I find vitamin B complex?
- White and wholemeal bread
- Fortified breakfast cereals
- Meat, liver, kidney

How can health be affected if there is not enough vitamin B complex?
- Tiredness due to energy not being released from the carbohydrates
- Depression, irritability, anxiety
- Slow growth in children

Two other vitamin B complex make an important contribution to good health.

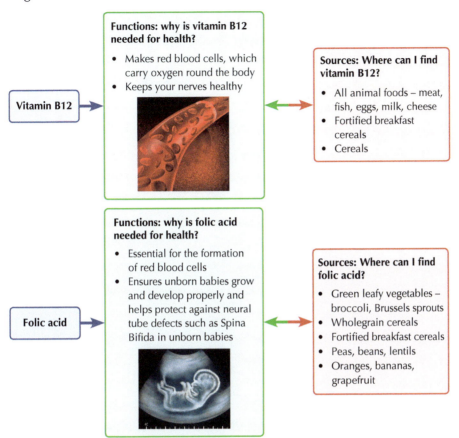

Vitamin B12

Functions: why is vitamin B12 needed for health?

- Makes red blood cells, which carry oxygen round the body
- Keeps your nerves healthy

Sources: Where can I find vitamin B12?

- All animal foods – meat, fish, eggs, milk, cheese
- Fortified breakfast cereals
- Cereals

Folic acid

Functions: why is folic acid needed for health?

- Essential for the formation of red blood cells
- Ensures unborn babies grow and develop properly and helps protect against neural tube defects such as Spina Bifida in unborn babies

Sources: Where can I find folic acid?

- Green leafy vegetables – broccoli, Brussels sprouts
- Wholegrain cereals
- Fortified breakfast cereals
- Peas, beans, lentils
- Oranges, bananas, grapefruit

The effect on health if the vitamin B12 and folic acid balance is not right

How can health be affected if there is not enough vitamin B12?

- You will **feel** tired and **listless** as your body won't be able to make as many red blood cells as normal.
- A type of **anaemia** called pernicious anaemia may develop.

How can health be affected if there is a not enough folic acid?

- Neural tube defects in unborn babies may develop – this is when the baby's spine and nervous system do not develop properly.
- A type of **anaemia** may develop called megaloblastic anaemia.

⚠ Watch point

Vitamin B12 is only found in useful amounts in animal foods. **Vegan vegetarians** who eat no animal foods are at risk of a deficiency and may require supplements.

✔ Test your knowledge

1. Describe one function of vitamin B complex.
2. State one effect on health of a vitamin B complex deficiency.
3. Identify one group of people who could be deficient in vitamin B12 and explain the reason for this.
4. Explain the function of folic acid and its effect on health.

Let's Cook

Time to make a dish which includes vitamin B complex.

Examples of dishes you could make:

1. Bread and butter pudding
2. Spicy naan bread pizza with tuna and spinach

Blackcurrants are a rich source of vitamin C.

Vitamin C

Functions: why do we need vitamin C?

1. To make connective tissue to bind the body cells together.
2. Helps cuts and wounds heal quicker.
3. It helps protect our immune system.
4. Assists in the absorption of iron to prevent anaemia.
5. To build and maintain the skin.

Vitamin C is an antioxidant vitamin (see page 23 for further information).

Sources: where can we find vitamin C?

Rich sources	Good sources
Blackcurrants	Citrus fruits (oranges, lemons, limes)
Green pepper	Strawberries
Kiwi	Green, leafy vegetables (spinach, cabbage)

The effect on health if vitamin C balance is not right

Not enough
Cuts and wounds fail to heal properly.
Anaemia may develop as vitamin C has to be present to allow iron to be absorbed.
There is a greater risk of developing cancer and heart disease in later life as vitamin C is an antioxidant vitamin.

Vitamin C acts as an antioxidant and prevents free radicals from doing damage to our cells.

Free radicals are molecules which damage body cells/tissues and puts us more at risk of developing cancers and coronary heart disease (CHD).

An important point to remember is that – because the body cannot store vitamin C – you should aim to eat vitamin C-rich foods daily.

🔍 Hint

Many products especially aimed at children are fortified with vitamin C.

☑ Test your knowledge

1. Give two functions of vitamin C.
2. What will happen if there is not enough vitamin C in the diet?
3. What are free radicals?
4. Describe two effects on health which result from a lack of vitamin C.

Let's Cook

Time to make a dish which includes vitamin C.

Examples of dishes you could make:

1. Fresh fruit salad to include vitamin C-rich fruits
2. Strawberry cheesecake
3. Spinach and ricotta cheese cannelloni

Antioxidant vitamins

What are they?

Antioxidants are substances that can be found in many foods.

Antioxidant vitamins have the following functions:

- They ward off free radicals, which are produced as a natural result of the oxygen using processes in the body, e.g. breathing, digestion.

- Antioxidants form a defence system against these free radicals which damage cells and tissues resulting in an increased risk of heart disease and cancers.

The most common antioxidant vitamins are vitamins A, C and E.

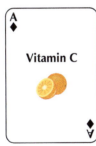
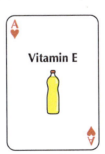

The antioxidant vitamins – vitamin A, vitamin C and vitamin E – spell out the word ACE. This is a good way to remember them.

Where can we find these antioxidants?

Antioxidants occur naturally in a wide range of foods.

- Vitamin A – red and orange fruit and vegetables, e.g. carrots, tomatoes, apricots and peaches.

- Vitamin C – citrus fruits, blackcurrants, kiwi fruit, green leafy vegetables, e.g. broccoli, spinach and cabbage.

- Vitamin E – vegetable oils, wholegrain cereals, green leafy vegetables.

 Hint

Antioxidants also help to build the immune system.

⚠ **Watch point**

Different antioxidants work in different ways so the key is to eat a variety of foods that include vitamins A, C and E.

☑ Test your knowledge

1. Name the antioxidant vitamins.
2. Describe two effects that antioxidant vitamins could have on health.
3. List two dishes which could supply a range of antioxidant vitamins and identify the ingredients containing them.

💭 Let's Cook

Time to make a dish which includes antioxidant vitamins.

Examples of dishes you could make:

1. Spinach and ricotta pizza
2. Blueberry muffins

The effects of storage, preparation and cooking on vitamins

Storage of vitamins

Vitamin	Effect	How to reduce the loss
Vitamin A	• Vitamin A is found in fatty foods and may be lost due to oxidation or exposure to light. Oxidation is where a food is exposed to the oxygen in the air, which results in the loss of water-soluble vitamins.	• Store in the fridge, cover foods, or store in dark containers away from the light.
Vitamin B complex		
Vitamin B1 (thiamine)	• Exposure to light/UV light reduces thiamine content.	• Store away from light.
Vitamin B2 (riboflavin)	• Deteriorates quickly with exposure to UV light, especially in supermarket chill cabinets, e.g. salad bags.	• Store away from sunlight, keep in dark conditions. • Avoid foods stored for a length of time in brightly lit supermarket display cabinets.
Vitamin B3 (niacin)	• Some loss due to oxidation.	• Avoid storage if possible.

Vitamin	Effect	How to reduce the loss
Vitamin C	• Vitamin C is lost through oxidation. • Exposure to air changes the chemical structure of vitamin C, resulting in it not being able to be used by the body. • Bruised fruits and vegetables lose vitamin C due to enzyme action and oxidation. • Ready-prepared produce has gone through processing which exposes the produce to air and light, reducing vitamin C content.	• Buy as fresh as possible. • Store in a refrigerator, as low temperature slows down oxidation, e.g. green vegetables in fridge. • Store away from the light, e.g. root vegetables such as potatoes in a cool dark cupboard. • Avoid bruising or damage prior to storage. • Avoid buying ready-prepared produce as it is more likely to have suffered nutrient loss. • Frozen vegetables have a higher vitamin C content because they are frozen quickly to preserve the vitamin.

Preparation of vitamins

Vitamin	Effect	How to reduce the loss
Vitamin B complex	• Vitamin B is found in the bran (outer husk) of a cereal. When the wheat is milled to produce white flour this bran is removed resulting in the loss of vitamin B. • White rice is usually polished to remove the bran, which results in the vitamin B being lost.	• Buy wholegrain bread or brown rice.
Vitamin C	• Vitamin C is very unstable and, being water-soluble, can easily leach into any liquid it is in. • Exposure to light reduces the vitamin C content through oxidation. • An enzyme in vegetables called **oxidase** is activated by chopping and cutting. • Peeling exposes the surface to air, speeding up oxidation.	• Avoid soaking in water. • Do not prepare too far in advance. • Use sharp knives to reduce damage to the cells as this causes the enzyme to be released. • Avoid peeling if possible or peel thinly, as most vitamin C is just under the skin. • Use acids such as lemon juice to slow down the loss of vitamin C through oxidation.

Cooking of vitamins

Vitamin	Effect	How to reduce the loss
Vitamin B complex	• Vitamin B is stable in temperatures up to boiling point. It is gradually destroyed if heated to above boiling point for a long period of time. • Folic acid is water-soluble and destroyed by prolonged cooking.	• Use quick methods of cooking such as steaming, stir-frying, microwaving and pressure cooking to preserve the vitamin.
Vitamin C	• Destroyed by very low temperatures. • Is lost through leaching into water. • Prolonged cooking leads to vitamin C being lost through leaching or exposure to heat. • Can be lost by reheating foods or keeping foods warm.	• Add to boiling water and cook for the minimum time. • Use as little water as possible to prevent loss through leaching. • Choose cooking methods such as microwaving and stir-frying to reduce this loss. • Cook for as short a time as possible. • Serve immediately.

⚠ Watch point

Microwaved and steamed vegetables do not require any salt to be added as these methods of cooking bring out the natural flavours of the vegetables.

Let's Cook

Time to make a dish which shows the effects of preparation, storage and cooking on vitamins.

Examples of dishes you could make:

1. Summer fruit salad
2. Vegetable pasta salad
3. Strawberry and blackcurrant layer cake

✔ Test your knowledge

1. State two methods to prevent the loss of vitamin A during storage.
2. List one way to prevent the loss of vitamin B complex during cooking.
3. Identify and explain two ways to prevent the loss of vitamin C during the storage of green vegetables.
4. Describe two ways to prevent losing vitamin C during the cooking of vegetables.

Topic 3: Micro-nutrients: minerals – calcium, iron, phosphorus and sodium

Minerals: what are they and where do we get them?

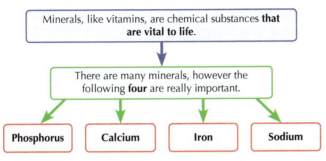

Minerals, like vitamins, are chemical substances **that are vital to life**.

There are many minerals, however the following **four** are really important.

| Phosphorus | Calcium | Iron | Sodium |

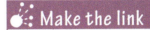 **Make the link**

See topic 5 on the inter-relationship of nutrients.

Calcium

Functions: why do we need calcium?

1. It combines with phosphorous to make calcium phosphate, which gives hardness and strength to bones and teeth.
2. Required for the maintenance of bones and teeth.
3. Helps to prevent osteoporosis in later life.
4. Helps blood to clot after injury.
5. Required for the correct functioning of muscles and nerves.

Hint

Calcium is more effective when taken in smaller doses spread throughout the day as it ensures a constant supply.

Sources: where can we find calcium?

- Milk, cheese, yoghurt
- Fortified white flour
- Green leafy vegetables
- Tinned fish, e.g. sardines, salmon
- Dried fruit, nuts, cereals

⚠ Watch point

Children and teenagers need the most calcium because this is their 'peak' time for bone development. See Chapter 3, topic 2, on teenagers' dietary reference values (DRVs).

The effect on health if calcium balance is not right

Not enough
Low intake over a period of time may lead to poor development of bones (leading to rickets – soft bones) and teeth (leading to dental caries).
If a bone is broken or damaged then it may take longer to heal if calcium is lacking.
Osteoporosis (brittle bones) in later life.
Osteomalacia (adult rickets).
Blood loss, as it does clot well after an injury.

Let's Cook

Time to make a dish which includes calcium.

Examples of dishes you could make:

1. Cream of broccoli soup
2. Salmon fishcakes

✔ Test your knowledge

1. Name four sources of calcium.
2. Explain two functions of calcium in the diet.
3. Describe the effects on health is if there is not enough calcium in the diet.

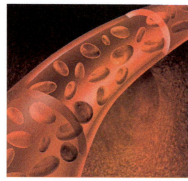

Haemoglobin helps to transport oxygen around the body to every cell.

Iron

Functions: why do we need iron?

1. Iron is a component of haemoglobin, the substance that forms red blood cells.
2. Haemoglobin helps to transport oxygen around the body to every cell to help reduce the feeling of tiredness.
3. Iron is required to prevent anaemia.

Sources: where can we find iron?

- Red meat, especially liver, kidney, corned beef

- Fortified flour and bread

- Green leafy vegetables

- Dried fruit and pulses

- Cocoa and plain chocolate

- Eating fresh fruit or salad vegetables (including tomatoes) or drinking fruit juice (all of which contain vitamin C) with meals helps the body absorb the iron in food.

⚠ Watch point

Beef is one of the richest sources of iron. A 100-gram serving of lean beef provides almost four times as much iron as a cup of raw spinach.

🔍 Hint

Cutting down on tea could help to improve iron levels in the body because it contains a substance (tannin) which can bind with iron, making it harder for the body to absorb it.

The effect on health if the iron balance is not right

Not enough	Too much
Tiredness, lacking in energy, weakness	Too much iron can collect mainly in the liver and can be toxic (poisonous)
Anaemia	

Special requirements

- **Pregnant women** – iron requirements increase during pregnancy to allow for the development of the growing baby's blood supply.

- **Girls and women** – regular menstrual loss of blood means that the iron lost during this time needs to be replaced.

- **Injuries and operations** – the iron in the blood lost needs to be replaced.

- **Babies** – babies are born with a supply of iron to last them up to four months as milk contains very little iron.

⚠ Watch point

Iron tablets must be stored out of the reach of children as they can be dangerous if taken in large quantities.

☕ Let's Cook

Time to make a dish which includes iron.

Examples of dishes you could make:

1. Meatballs with spaghetti
2. Vegetable curry with chickpeas
3. Lentil soup with wholemeal rolls

✔ Test your knowledge

1. Explain two functions of iron in the diet.
2. Identify two groups of people most at risk from an iron deficiency and explain why.
3. Name two foods rich in iron.

Phosphorus

Functions: why do we need phosphorus?

1. Works with calcium in the formation, development and maintenance of strong bones.
2. Works along with calcium to form strong bones and teeth.

Sources: where can we find phosphorus?

- Milk, cheese, yoghurt
- Bread and cereal products
- Meat and meat products
- Fish
- Nuts

Milk is a good source of phosphorus.

The effect on health if the phosphorus balance is not right

Not enough
People are rarely deficient in phosphorus, but insufficient amounts could affect the body's ability to build and maintain healthy bones.

Sodium

Functions: why do we need sodium?

1. Essential for maintaining the correct fluid balance in the body.
2. Required for correct muscle and nerve activity – too low an intake can lead to muscle cramps.

Sources: where can we find sodium?

- Table salt
- Salty snacks
- Canned foods
- Takeaway meals

Many processed foods and Chinese meals are high in monosodium glutamate (MSG), a flavour enhancer which is high in sodium.

Deficiencies: what will happen if I don't get enough sodium?

The effect on health if the sodium balance is not right

Not enough	Too much
People are rarely deficient in sodium but muscle cramps may occur, especially after exercise.	High blood pressure, strokes and coronary heart disease.

Other minerals are also important such as:

- Potassium as it helps to control blood pressure.
- Magnesium as it is involved with the formation of bones.

⚠ Watch point

You don't have to add salt to food to be eating too much: 75% of the salt we eat is already in everyday foods such as bread, breakfast cereal and ready meals. Adults should be eating no more than 6g of salt per day (one teaspoon), children should be eating less.
Log on to the following website and watch the video clip entitled 'Say No to Salt': www.nhs.uk/Livewell/Goodfood/Pages/salt.aspx#adult

✔ Test your knowledge

1. Research the following: sodium versus salt – what's the difference?
2. State the effect on health of having a diet high in salt.

Topic 4: Water and dietary fibre

Water

Functions: why do we need water?

1. Vital to life – it is required for all body fluids, e.g. saliva, digestive juices, blood, sweat, urine.
2. Helps excrete waste from the body as it combines with NSP to prevent constipation.
3. Regulates body temperature through perspiration.
4. Lubricates joints and membranes.

Sources: where can we find water?

- Fruit and vegetables
- Milk/fruit juices
- Tap water/bottled water

Deficiencies: what will happen if we don't get enough water?

You may become dehydrated, which could result in confusion and lack of concentration.

Water provides a number of benefits when dieting – if you're hungry, you can have a glass of water. It has zero calories and it helps to fill your stomach and suppress your appetite. Water also helps to flush out toxins from the body.

As our bodies are made up of mostly water, we can go longer without food than we can without water, as the body requires water to run efficiently.

> 🔍 **Hint**
>
> One of the easiest and most effective ways to help your diet is to drink water, however water can also be taken in through other types of drinks and foods with a high water content, e.g. melon, soups.

Dietary fibre, also known as fibre, Non Starch Polysaccharides (NSP)

Functions: why do we need dietary fibre?

1. Helps to remove toxic or harmful waste products from the body.
2. Helps prevents bowel disorders such as constipation, diverticular disease and bowel cancer.
3. Absorbs water to help bulk out faeces, which helps it move through the body.
4. Gives a feeling of fullness, to help prevent overeating and obesity.
5. May help to lower LDL cholesterol and so reduce the risk of heart disease.

Sources: where can we find dietary fibre?

- Wholegrain cereals, bread, oats
- Pulse vegetables – peas, beans, lentils
- Fresh fruit and vegetabes

There are two types of dietary fibre:

1. **Soluble fibre**
   This type is thought to slow down digestion and absorption of carbohydrates to help control blood sugar level – useful for diabetics.

2. **Insoluble fibre**
   This type absorbs water and increases bulk to help the gut work properly.

Deficiencies: What is the effect on health if I don't have enough dietary fibre in my diet?

- Bowel disorders, e.g. constipation, bowel cancer.

Let's Cook

Time to make a dish which includes water and dietary fibre.

Examples of dishes you could make:

1. Cream of vegetable soup
2. Ratatouille with pasta
3. Poached pears with raspberry coulis

✔ Test your knowledge

1. State the function of water in the diet.
2. How much water should an adult have every day?
3. Explain the difference between insoluble and soluble fibre.
4. Describe two effects on health of having insufficient dietary fibre in the diet.

Topic 5: Absorption and inter-relationship of nutrients

Calcium and iron absorption

Factors that affect the absorption of calcium:

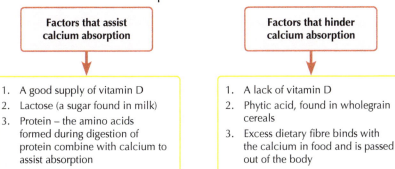

Factors that assist calcium absorption

1. A good supply of vitamin D
2. Lactose (a sugar found in milk)
3. Protein – the amino acids formed during digestion of protein combine with calcium to assist absorption

Factors that hinder calcium absorption

1. A lack of vitamin D
2. Phytic acid, found in wholegrain cereals
3. Excess dietary fibre binds with the calcium in food and is passed out of the body

Factors that affect the absorption of iron:

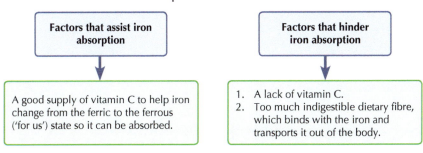

Factors that assist iron absorption

A good supply of vitamin C to help iron change from the ferric to the ferrous ('for us') state so it can be absorbed.

Factors that hinder iron absorption

1. A lack of vitamin C.
2. Too much indigestible dietary fibre, which binds with the iron and transports it out of the body.

Inter-relationship of nutrients

Many nutrients have to inter-relate, or work together, in order to be able to function properly.

CALCIUM   PHOSPHORUS

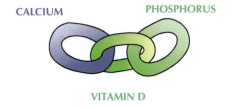

VITAMIN D

Calcium and phosphorus are both needed together for the formation and maintenance of strong bones and teeth. Together they form **calcium phosphate**, which gives bones and teeth their hardness. Vitamin D is the 'essential link'.

VITAMIN C

FOLIC ACID   IRON

> ⚠ **Watch point**
>
> Vitamins are the 'essential link' in the chain to make sure the other nutrients work efficiently.

> **Make the link**
>
> Look at individual nutrients throughout this chapter.

Depending on the food source, only 10% of the iron eaten is actually absorbed by the body. Iron in our food is in the 'ferric' state and cannot be absorbed until it is changed to the 'ferrous' state, e.g. if there is a shortage of iron in the diet, folic acid takes over the role and helps prevent anaemia. Vitamin C acts as the nutcracker required to change the iron into this state. Where iron is low, however, folic acid takes over the nutcracker role. If there is a shortage of iron in the diet, folic acid takes over the role and helps to prevent anaemia.

Vitamin B complex and carbohydrates also work together: vitamin B helps release the energy from carbohydrate foods.

Vitamin B complex and carbohydrates also work together: vitamin B helps release energy from carbohydrate foods.

Deficiencies: what will happen if I don't get the balance of these nutrients right?

You run the risk of becoming deficient in those nutrients (refer to topics 1 and 2 in this chapter).

☑ Test your knowledge

1. Describe how calcium, phosphorus and vitamin D work together.
2. Which nutrient helps the absorption of iron?
3. State two factors that:
    a. assist calcium absorption
    b. hinder calcium absorption.

Let's Cook

Time to make a dish to link the nutrients together.

Examples of dishes you could make:

1. Cottage pie
2. Chilli meatballs
3. Pasta with a creamy spinach and pine nut sauce

GO! End of chapter activities

Activity 1
Keep a food diary for a week

Investigate the amount of protein, carbohydrate and fat you need for your body and make up a diet plan to ensure you get just the right amount. (Refer to Chapter 1, topic 2 to help you.)

Arrange the foods you have eaten into the following table:

Macro-nutrients					
Protein		Carbohydrates		Fats	
HBV	LBV	Starches	Sugars	Saturated	Unsaturated

Evaluate your diet linked to your findings. A copy of this table can be downloaded from www.leckieandleckie.co.uk/n45health

Activity 2
In pairs

1. Carry out further investigation into the role of antioxidant vitamins and develop a consumer information poster for the doctor's surgery on the value of antioxidants in the diet.

2. Carry out further investigation on the role of folic acid in the diet and develop an information leaflet for the ante-natal clinic on the value of folic acid before and during pregnancy.

Activity 3
Working on your own

Develop a children's bookmark to hand out to the local primary school to inform children of the importance of vitamin C in the diet and how they could make sure they are getting enough of it.

Activity 4
Working on your own

Develop a Top Tips app for a smartphone on the importance of micro-nutrients for teenagers.

Activity 5
Group task

Carry out a nutritional comparison of a range of breakfast cereals and report your findings back to the class.

Write up an evaluation of the findings to include information on energy, fat, protein, mineral and vitamin content.

Activity 6
Group task

Carry out a nutritional analysis of a home-made dish and compare it to the nutritional information of the same dish produced commercially, e.g. macaroni cheese or spaghetti bolognese.

❓ Exam-style questions

To help you with exam technique, remember to look at page 191–202, Keeping on track: preparing for the National 5 course assessment.

Question 1
Name **two** nutrients which can be found in wholemeal bread and explain at least **one** function of **each** in the diet.   **4 marks**

Question 2
Explain the inter-relationship between calcium and vitamin D.   **1 mark**

Question 3
Describe **one** way to help prevent the loss of **vitamin C** from **vegetables** during **each** of the following stages:

a) Storage   b) Preparation   c) Cooking   **3 marks**

Question 4
State **two** functions of salt in the diet and give **two** practical ways to reduce salt in the diet.   **4 marks**

Now check your answers at the back of the book.

Rate your progress

How confident are you that you have achieved each of the following objectives?

Using the following key as a guide, give yourself a rating for each of the objectives below

Rating	Explanation
1	Confident with the standard of my work
2	Fairly confident with the standard of my work
3	The majority of my work was satisfactory
4	Require to do some further work
5	Require a lot of work

Objectives	Rating
Explain the function and effects on health of the macro-nutrients: protein, fat and carbohydrates	
Explain the function and effects on health of the micro-nutrients vitamins and minerals	
Explain the function and effects on health of water and dietary fibre	
Explain the inter-relationship of nutrients	
Describe the effects of storage, preparation and cooking on nutrients	

Look at your ratings.

Write down two **next steps** to 'unlocking' your knowledge of food and health.

2 Current dietary advice

After completing this chapter you should be able to:

- Describe in detail current dietary advice.
- Select and use appropriate ingredients, food products and cooking methods to meet the dietary and health needs.
- Explain how food products meet the dietary and health needs of individuals.

Make the Link

Throughout this chapter refer to Chapter 3.

Topic 1: Scottish dietary goals

Dietary goals: what are they and why do we need them?

The dietary goals form a basis for addressing the increasing number of deficiencies in the Scottish diet.

There are eight dietary goals:

Fruit and Vegetables: average intake of a variety of fruit and vegetables to reach at least five portions or 400g per day. ✓

Fibre/dietary fibre: increase average intake to 18g per day by increasing consumption of wholegrains, e.g. bread, breakfast cereals, pulses and vegetables. ✓

Oily fish: increase intake to one 140g portion per week. ✓

Calories: Reduce calorie intake by 120 calories per person per day. Reduce energy density intake by replacing high fat and/or sugary products with starchy carbohydrates or complex carbohydrates, such as bread, pasta, rice, potatoes, fruit and vegetables. ✗

Fat: average intake of total fat to reduce to no more than 35% of food energy. Average intake of saturated fats to reduce to no more than 11% of food energy. Average intake of trans-fatty acids to remain below 1% of food energy.

Salt: average sodium intake to reduce to 6g per day (approx. 1 tsp).

Sugar: average intake of Non Milk Extrinsic (NME) sugars to reduce to less than 11% of food energy in children and adults. NME sugars are found in sweets, biscuits, soft drinks and added to lots of processed foods, such as sauces and soups.

Red Meat: Average intake of red and processed meat, e.g. sausages and burgers, to be around 70g per day.
Consumers who have a high intake of red and processed meats (90g per day) should not increase their intake.

Contribution of the dietary goals to good health

The following **diet-related** conditions:
- bowel disorders
- bowel cancer
- constipation

can be prevented by following the dietary goals below.

1. Increase intake of fruit and vegetables, as they are good sources of fibre.
2. Increase intake of fibre.

Fibre bulks up faeces and helps them to pass through the system.

3. Reduce intake of red and processed meats, as they are linked to an increased risk of bowel and stomach cancer.

The following **diet-related** conditions:
- high blood pressure (HBP)
- obesity
- coronary heart disease (CHD)

can be prevented by following the dietary goals below.

1. Increase intake of fruit and vegetables
2. Increase intake of fibre

High-fibre foods fill you up and prevent you snacking on junk food which is high in fat, salt and sugar. Fruit and vegetables also provide a good supply of ACE vitamins which destroy the free radicals that cause heart disease and cancers.

3. Increase intake of oily fish

Oily fish is high in Omega 3 fatty acids, which may help to reduce the risk of blood clots and lower the risk of CHD.

4. Reduce calorie intake
5. Reduce sugar intake
6. Reduce fat intake

Less fat will be stored in the body, which reduces the risk of obesity, HBP and CHD. A high intake of saturated fat may raise cholesterol in the blood and lead to a narrowing of the arteries and an increased risk of CHD.

7. Reduce salt intake, as this reduces the risk of HBP.

8. Reduce red meat intake, as it can be high in fat and processed meats can be high in salt.

The **diet-related** condition **anaemia** can be prevented by following the dietary goals below, as they supply a good source of **iron**.

1. Eat red meat, but choose lean meat and don't exceed 70g per day.
2. Increase intake of fruit and vegetables, particularly dark leafy greens such a spinach.
3. Eat starchy carbohydrates rich in iron, such as wholegrains and beans.

🔍 Hint

- Eating white fish can help reduce obesity if cooked without fat.
- Eating oily fish can lower the risk of heart disease.

The following dietary goals are rich in protein, which is essential for **growth**, **repair** and **maintenance** of the body.

1. Increase intake of oily fish, such as salmon or tuna.
2. Eat red meat, but choose lean meat and don't exceed 70g per day.
3. Increase intake of fibre from wholegrains and pulses.

The following dietary goals are rich in calcium, which is essential for **building** and **maintaining strong bones** and **teeth**.

1. Increase intake of oily fish, such as sardines and pilchards.
2. Increase intake of fibre by eating starchy carbohydrates, which are often fortified with calcium.
3. Increase intake of vegetables, particularly green leafy veg such as broccoli and cabbage.
4. Eat reduced fat dairy products, such as semi-skimmed milk.

The following dietary goals are good sources of folic acid, which is essential for reducing the risk of babies developing spina bifida during pregnancy.

1. Increase intake of fruit and vegetables, such as spinach, kale, oranges and orange juice.
2. Increase intake of fibre by eating lentils, wholegrains and breakfast cereals fortified with folic acid.

Sugar
High sugar intake is linked to tooth decay and a greater risk of developing type 2 diabetes.

Salt
High salt intake may contribute to stomach cancer and lead to kidney problems in children.

Sugar substitutes, low-fat spreads and salt alternatives have been developed to help reduce the effects of a diet too high in fat, salt and sugar.

✔ Test your knowledge

1. List three foods we should eat to help meet each of the dietary goals.
2. Which dietary goal supplies antioxidant vitamins?
3. How much fat, salt and sugar should we be consuming?
4. Explain the dangers of diets that are high in fat, salt and/or sugar.
5. Which dietary goals do we need to increase?

Let's Cook

Time to make a dish to meet the dietary goals.

1. Low-fat cheesecake – reduces fat intake.
2. Apple and cinnamon scones – increases fruit and dietary fibre intake.
3. Herb crusted chicken with pasta – increases dietary fibre intake.
4. Chicken tikka kebab with rice – reduces fat and salt intake.

Topic 2: Practical ways of using ingredients to meet the dietary goals

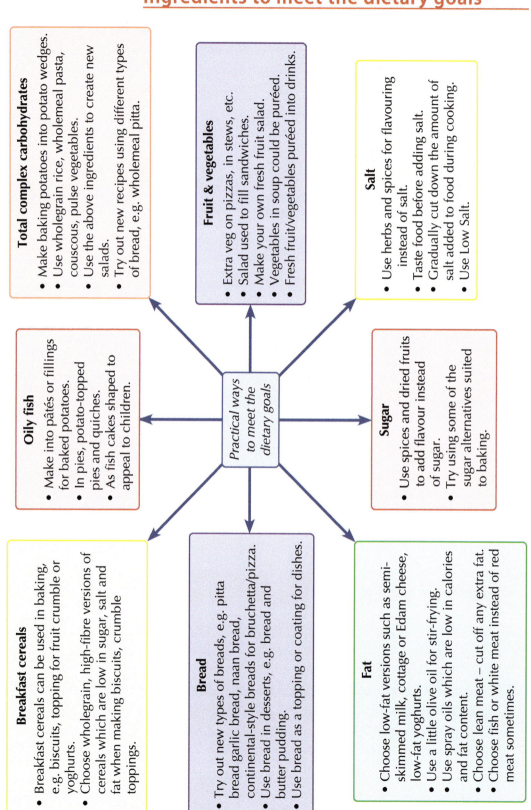

Total complex carbohydrates
- Make baking potatoes into potato wedges.
- Use wholegrain rice, wholemeal pasta, couscous, pulse vegetables.
- Use the above ingredients to create new salads.
- Try out new recipes using different types of bread, e.g. wholemeal pitta.

Fruit & vegetables
- Extra veg on pizzas, in stews, etc.
- Salad used to fill sandwiches.
- Make your own fresh fruit salad.
- Vegetables in soup could be puréed.
- Fresh fruit/vegetables puréed into drinks.

Salt
- Use herbs and spices for flavouring instead of salt.
- Taste food before adding salt.
- Gradually cut down the amount of salt added to food during cooking.
- Use Low Salt.

Oily fish
- Make into pâtés or fillings for baked potatoes.
- In pies, potato-topped pies and quiches.
- As fish cakes shaped to appeal to children.

Practical ways to meet the dietary goals

Sugar
- Use spices and dried fruits to add flavour instead of sugar.
- Try using some of the sugar alternatives suited to baking.

Breakfast cereals
- Breakfast cereals can be used in baking, e.g. biscuits, topping for fruit crumble or yoghurts.
- Choose wholegrain, high-fibre versions of cereals which are low in sugar, salt and fat when making biscuits, crumble toppings.

Bread
- Try out new types of breads, e.g. pitta bread garlic bread, naan bread, continental-style breads for bruchetta/pizza.
- Use bread in desserts, e.g. bread and butter pudding.
- Use bread as a topping or coating for dishes.

Fat
- Choose low-fat versions such as semi-skimmed milk, cottage or Edam cheese, low-fat yoghurts.
- Use a little olive oil for stir-frying.
- Use spray oils which are low in calories and fat content.
- Choose lean meat – cut off any extra fat.
- Choose fish or white meat instead of red meat sometimes.

Topic 2: Practical ways of using cooking methods to meet the dietary goals

Stir-frying
Small pieces of food cooked quickly in very little oil. Less loss of vitamins B and C as the food is not overcooked or submerged in liquid. Also the recommended type of meat is lean.

Poaching
Gentle cooking of food, **just below boiling point, in the required amount of liquid**. It is healthier as **no fat is added** and the liquid could be made into a sauce or coulis to serve with the food such as fish, fruit and eggs.

Steaming
Cooking of food by steam from boiling water. Steaming is healthier than other cooking methods as no fat or salt is added and because the food is not submerged, essential vitamins are not leached into the water. Good for cooking fish, vegetables and chicken.

Baking
Food is cooked by **dry heat**. It is healthier as **no added fat** is used and a range of ingredients such as chicken, fish, fruit, vegetables, baked products, milk puddings can be cooked this way.

Practical ways to meet the dietary goals

Pressure cooking
Cooking of food in a special pan which cooks under pressure. The water boils at a higher temperature, forcing steam through the food cooking it very quickly. Good for making casseroles/stews, soup and milk puddings.

Grilling
Fast method of cooking using intense heat **radiated** over the food. It is healthier as **little or no fat is used and and any fat in the food drips out**. A variety of foods can be grilled, such as lean meat, vegetables and bread.

Microwaving
A healthy alternative to using the cooker. No fat or water is needed as the water molecules in the food vibrate due to the microwaves and causes cooking through friction.

Hints
✓ Baked or boiled potatoes are healthier than chips.
✓ Cut off any extra fat before cooking.
✓ Gradually cut down the amount of salt added to food during cooking.
✓ Use a little olive oil for stir-frying as this is a mono-unsaturated fat and will help keep cholesterol levels down.
✓ Use a spray-on fat for frying.
✓ Add noodles to a stir-fry.

Topic 2: Make the correct choice from the supermarket shelves

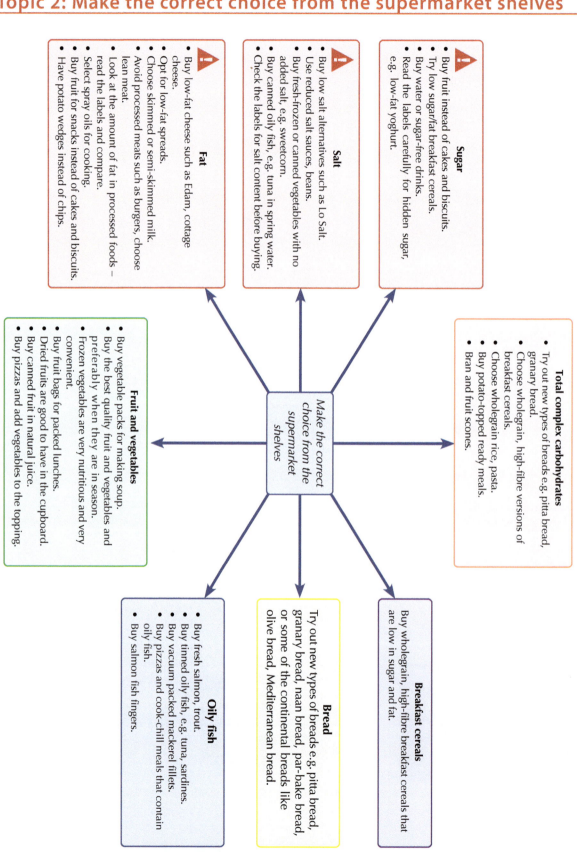

Sugar

• Buy fruit instead of cakes and biscuits.
• Try low sugar/fat breakfast cereals.
• Buy water or sugar-free drinks.
• Read the labels carefully for hidden sugar, e.g. low-fat yoghurt.

Salt

• Buy low salt alternatives such as Lo Salt.
• Use reduced salt sauces, beans.
• Buy fresh-frozen or canned vegetables with no added salt, e.g. sweetcorn.
• Buy canned oily fish, e.g. tuna in spring water.
• Check the labels for salt content before buying.

Fat

• Buy low-fat cheese such as Edam, cottage cheese.
• Opt for low-fat spreads.
• Choose skimmed or semi-skimmed milk.
• Avoid processed meats such as burgers, choose lean meat.
• Look at the amount of fat in processed foods – read the labels and compare.
• Select spray oils for cooking.
• Buy fruit for snacks instead of cakes and biscuits.
• Have potato wedges instead of chips.

Total complex carbohydrates

• Try out new types of breads e.g. pitta bread, granary bread.
• Choose wholegrain, high-fibre versions of breakfast cereals.
• Choose wholegrain rice, pasta.
• Buy potato-topped ready meals.
• Bran and fruit scones.

Make the correct choice from the supermarket shelves

Fruit and vegetables

• Buy vegetable packs for making soup.
• Buy the best quality fruit and vegetables and preferably when they are in season.
• Frozen vegetables are very nutritious and very convenient.
• Buy fruit bags for packed lunches.
• Dried fruits are good to have in the cupboard.
• Buy canned fruit in natural juice.
• Buy pizzas and add vegetables to the topping.

Oily fish

• Buy fresh salmon, trout.
• Buy tinned oily fish, e.g. tuna, sardines.
• Buy vacuum packed mackerel fillets.
• Buy pizzas and cook-chill meals that contain oily fish.
• Buy salmon fish fingers.

Bread

Try out new types of breads e.g. pitta bread, granary bread, naan bread, par-bake bread, or some of the continental breads like olive bread, Mediterranean bread.

Breakfast cereals

Buy wholegrain, high-fibre breakfast cereals that are low in sugar and fat.

✔ Test your knowledge

1. Give five recommendations of what to buy in the supermarket to help meet the dietary goals.

2. Explain how the correct choice of ingredients can help us meet each of the dietary goals.

3. For each of the cooking methods listed on page 41 explain how they contribute to the dietary goals.

Let's Cook

Time to make a dish to meet the dietary goals.

1. Take a recipe you have made before and adapt it by including ingredients to improve the dietary goals. Explain what goals you have helped to meet.

2. Using a recipe you have made before, change the cooking method to make it healthier.

3. Adapt a basic macaroni cheese recipe to make it healthier and to meet at least one of the dietary goals.

GO! End of chapter activities

Activity 1
Working on your own

Create your own infograph or mind map on the dietary goals as a revision tool.

Activity 2
In a group

Take a different dietary goal each and come up with a starter, main course, dessert and baked product which meets the goal.

As a class build all the recipes into a class recipe book.

If time allows, try out and photograph some of the recipes for the book.

Activity 3
In pairs

Carry out a comparison of a range of cereal bars and write up a report with the title 'Healthy or not healthy, the mystery behind the cereal bar'.

Activity 4
Working on your own

Develop a set of warning labels that could be used to alert people to the fat, salt and sugar content of foods.

Activity 5
Working on your own

Investigate the value of including fish in the diet and develop a leaflet for the local fishmonger called 'Fish – its value and tips on how to include more in the diet'.

Activity 6
On your own

You have been asked to design a leaflet/poster or presentation for the parents of nursery school children. The parents are keen to ensure their children have a healthy diet.

You must include:

a. at least four pieces of current dietary advice

b. a detailed description of each piece of dietary advice

c. information on practical ways of including food to meet this dietary advice in their childrens' diets.

Do this task well if you are working on your own, as it could be kept for your portfolio of work.

❓ Exam-style questions

To help you prepare for the exam, remember to look at pages 191–202, Keeping on track: preparing for the National 5 course assessment.

Question 1
State **two** practical ways of reducing fat in the diet.   **2 marks**

Question 2
a) A manufacturer wishes to adapt the following recipe to help meet current dietary advice.

Haddock bake	
Ingredients	
Haddock fillet	Butter
Tomatoes	White flour
Whole milk	Salt

Describe **three** adaptations that could be made to the recipe and explain how each helps to meet a **different** piece of current dietary advice.   **6 marks**

Question 3
State **two practical ways** to increase bread consumption.   **2 marks**

Now check your answers at the back of the book.

Rate your progress

How confident are you that you have achieved each of the following objectives?

Using the following key as a guide, give yourself a rating for each of the objectives below

Rating	Explanation
1	Confident with the standard of my work
2	Fairly confident with the standard of my work
3	The majority of my work was satisfactory
4	Require to do some further work
5	Require a lot of work

Objectives	Rating
Describe in detail current dietary advice	
Select and use appropriate ingredients, food products and cooking methods to meet the dietary and health needs of individuals	
Explain how food products meet the dietary and health needs of individuals	

Look at your ratings.

Write down two **next steps** to 'unlocking' your knowledge of food and health.

3 Benefits to health of a balanced and varied diet

After completing this chapter you should be able to:

- Describe the benefits to health of a balanced and varied diet.
- Evaluate dietary reference values with reference to specific individuals.
- Explain the dietary and health needs of different individuals such as babies and infants, children, teenagers, adults, elderly, women during pregnancy and lactation, convalescents, vegetarians.
- Make food products to meet dietary and health needs of different individuals.
- Explain how food products meet these dietary and health needs of different individuals.

Make the Link

Throughout this chapter refer to Chapters 1 and 2.

Hint

All foods and drinks can be part of a balanced diet, so you don't have to give up the foods that are a real treat as long as you don't eat them too often.

Topic 1: The benefits to health of a balanced and varied diet

What is a balanced diet?

A balanced diet is one which:

- Provides all the essential nutrients in the correct proportion and quantities to meet our needs.
- Includes a variety of food which will provide us with all the essential nutrients.
- Provides the right amount of energy, water and NSP/dietary fibre.

What are the health benefits of a balanced diet?

A balanced and varied diet can:

- Help protect you from many diet-related illnesses such as obesity, high blood pressure, heart disease, diabetes, cancer and tooth decay.
- Provide the right amount of energy for activities and so help prevent you becoming overweight.
- Allow you to grow and have general good health.

It is important to remember that no single food provides all the nutrients. Look at the mind map of the tuna pizza below to see the different nutrients that are contained in the ingredients.

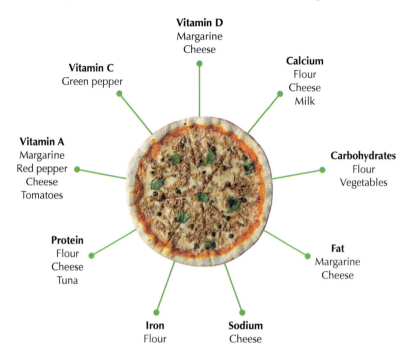

Vitamin D
Margarine
Cheese

Calcium
Flour
Cheese
Milk

Vitamin C
Green pepper

Carbohydrates
Flour
Vegetables

Vitamin A
Margarine
Red pepper
Cheese
Tomatoes

Protein
Flour
Cheese
Tuna

Fat
Margarine
Cheese

Iron
Flour

Sodium
Cheese

Make the Link

You may need to look back at Chapter 1 to help you.

Let's Cook

Make a savoury dish which could contribute to a balanced diet. You could make the dish you mind mapped in question 2 above.

Test your knowledge

1. **a)** Explain what is meant by a balanced diet.

   b) Describe the benefits to health of a balanced and varied diet.

2. Choose a savoury product such as lasagne. Thinking of the ingredients in your product identify the nutrients they contain. Present your information as a mind map.

3. Your friend is making sandwiches for her packed lunch. She has asked your opinion about which one would be the healthiest choice.

   • Cheddar cheese with pickle on a white roll.

   • Tuna, sweetcorn with low-fat mayonnaise on granary roll.

   • Crispy bacon, tomato, hard boiled egg on wholegrain roll.

   a) Choose one and give three reasons for your choice.

   b) Suggest two other additions to the packed lunch to make it balanced. Give a reason for each of your choices.

Topic 2: Dietary Reference Values (DRVs)

Our nutrient and energy needs will vary according to:

- Age
- Gender
- Body size – weight/height
- Lifestyle/physical activity
- Occupation
- Special circumstances such as pregnancy, lactation, illness, vegetarians, food allergies or intolerences

What are Dietary Reference Values?

Dietary reference values are one way of providing guidelines to help us have **a balanced diet**.

The nutritional needs of different individuals are measured by dietary reference values, as shown below.

Dietary Reference Values (DRVs)
are a series of figures for nutrients and energy which are enough or more to cover the needs of almost every healthy person in the country.
There are **three types** of values:

1. Reference Nutrient Intake (RNIs)	2. Estimated Average Requirements (EARs)	3. Lower Reference Nutrient Intake (LRNIs)
These are used for proteins, vitamins and minerals and should be enough for the needs of most people, even those with a high need of a nutrient. If individuals are consuming the RNI of a nutrient, they are unlikely to become deficient in that nutrient.	These are used mainly for energy intakes (but can also be used for nutrients). These figures give an estimate of the average amount of energy (or nutrient) needed. Some may need more, some may need less.	This is the amount of a nutrient that is enough for only a small amount of people with low needs. Most people would need more than the LRNI. If less than the LRNI amount was consumed over a period of time, then the person would become deficient in that nutrient.

Now let's look at some DRV figures in more detail

Energy

Estimated Average Requirements (EARs)

We get energy from protein, carbohydrate and fat in our diet.

Age	EAR MJ/day	
	Male	Female
1–3 years	5·15	4·86
4–6 years	7·16	6·46
7–10 years	8·24	7·28
11–14 years	9·27	7·92
15–18 years	11·51	8·83
19–49 years	10·60	8·10
50–59 years	10·60	8·00
60–64 years	9·93	7·99
65–74 years	9·71	7·96
75+ years	8·77	7·61

Source: Dietary Reference Values – A Guide, *HMSO*

Energy will be shown in MJ in DRV charts, but you will also see the energy content of food measured in calories or kJ on food labelling, recipes, magazine articles.

Remember that EARs are only average amounts.

Some people may need less energy	Some people may need more energy
People who do not take exercise or who have a job that does not use a lot of energy. 	Very active people such as athletes. People with a job that uses a lot of energy. 
Convalescents or invalids who are less active as they recover from an illness.	
People who are trying to reduce weight sensibly.	

You may see the following two abbreviations linked to your health:

BMR – Basal Metabolic Rate. This is the rate that energy is used when the body is at rest. This energy is needed to keep the body functioning, e.g. breathing, digestion.

BMI – Body Mass Index is a method for estimating body fat. Your BMI figure can tell you if you are underweight, of normal weight, overweight or obese.

Protein

Reference Nutrient Intake (RNIs)

Age	Reference Nutrient Intake (g/day)	
	Male	Female
1–3 years	14·5	14·5
4–6 years	19·7	19·7
7–10 years	28·3	28·3
11–14 years	42·1	42·1
15–18 years	55·2	45·0
19–50 years	55·5	45·0
50+ years	53·3	46·5
Pregnancy		+6
Lactation		
0–4 months		+11
4+ months		+8

Source: Dietary Reference Values – A Guide, *HMSO*

> **⚠ Watch point**
>
> Protein will be used as a secondary source of energy rather than for growth and repair if there is not enough in the diet. Compare the energy figures carefully with the amount of protein in the DRV question.

Minerals

Reference Nutrient Intake (RNIs)

Reference Nutrient Intakes for minerals (per day)				
Age	Calcium mg	Phosphorous mg	Sodium g	Iron mg
1–3 years	350	270	0·5	6·9
4–6 years	450	350	0·7	6·1
7–10 years	550	450	1·2	8·7
Males				
11–14 years	1000	775	1·6	11·3
15–18 years	1000	775	1·6	11·3
19–50 years	700	550	1·6	8·7
50+ years	700	550	1·6	8·7
Females				
11–14 years	800	625	1·6	14·8*
15–18 years	800	625	1·6	14·8*
19–50 years	700	550	1·6	14·8*
50+ years	700	550	1·6	8·7
Pregnancy	*	*	*	*
Lactation				
0–4 months	+550	+440	*	*
4+ months	+550	+440	*	*

Source: Dietary Reference Values – A Guide, *HMSO.*

No additional calcium and iron should be needed during pregnancy unless it is an adolescent who is pregnant as her bones are still forming and her diet may be low in iron.

Vitamins

Reference Nutrient Intake (RNIs)

Reference Nutrient Intakes for vitamins (per day)								
Age	Thiamine vitamin B1 mg	Riboflavin vitamin B2 mg	Niacin (nicotinic acid equivalent) mg	Vitamin B12 µg	Folate µg	Vitamin C mg	Vitamin A µg	Vitamin D µg
1–3 years	0·5	0·6	8	0·5	70	30	400	7
4–6 years	0·7	0·8	11	0·8	100	30	500	7
7–10 years	0·7	1·0	12	1·0	150	30	500	–
Males								
11–14 years	0·9	1·2	15	1·2	200	35	600	–
15–18 years	1·1	1·3	18	1·5	200	40	700	–
19–50 years	1·0	1·3	17	1·5	200	40	700	–
50+ years	0·9	1·3	16	1·5	200	40	700	**

Reference Nutrient Intakes for vitamins (per day)								
Age	Thiamine vitamin B1 mg	Riboflavin vitamin B2 mg	Niacin (nicotinic acid equivalent) mg	Vitamin B12 μg	Folate μg	Vitamin C mg	Vitamin A μg	Vitamin D μg
Females								
11–14 years	0·7	1·1	12	1·2	200	35	600	–
15–18 years	0·8	1·1	14	1·5	200	40	600	–
19–50 years	0·8	1·1	13	1·5	200	40	600	–
50+ years	0·8	1·1	12	1·5	200	40	600	**
Pregnancy	+0·1	+0·3	*	*	+100	+10	+100	10
Lactation								
0–4 months	+0·2	+0·5	+2	+0·5	+60	+30	+350	10
4+ months	+0·2	+0·5	+2	+0·5	+60	+30	+350	10

Source: Dietary Reference Values – A Guide, *HMSO*

A growing number of people have been found to be lacking in vitamin D due to a lack of sunshine so have therefore been recommended to take a vitamin D supplement.

Fats and carbohydrates

DRVs for fat and carbohydrates are given as percentages of total food intake.

Fats

- **Total fat** should provide no more than **35% of total energy intake**.
- **Saturated fats** should provide no more than **11% of total energy intake**.

Carbohydrates

- Total carbohydrate intake should provide an average of **47% of total energy** intake.
- **37%** should be from **starches**.
- **10%** should be from **sugars**.

Guideline Daily Amounts

The **guideline daily amounts** (GDAs) will tell you that you should have approximately 70g fat (of which 20g is saturated) and 90g sugars per day.

The GDA for **fibre** is based on an estimated average intake of 18g.

> ⚠ **Watch point**
>
> It is a good idea to memorise the GDA for fibre. The easy way is to remember the amount is to think of the age you get to vote (18).

Let's Cook

Prepare a dish which would give a good supply of protein, carbohydrates and iron, e.g. chilli con carne, spaghetti bolognese.

If you can, use a computer programme to analyse the dish for nutritional content.

Did the dish have a good supply of the three nutrients?

✔ Test your knowledge

1. Look at the DRV charts to help you answer the following questions.
   a. What does EAR stand for?
   b. How many grams of protein are required by:
      i. A boy 15–18 years old.
      ii. A girl 15–18 years old.

   Explain why they are different.

   a. How much extra folic acid is needed during pregnancy? Why is this?
   b. How much iron is required by:
      i. A female aged 11–14 years old.
      ii. A female aged 50 and over.

   Explain why they are different.

   a. How much energy is required by:
      i. A male aged 15–18 years old.
      ii. A male aged 75 and over.

   Explain why they are different.

2. Look at the RNIs for the following three nutrients: protein; vitamin C; vitamin B1. Explain what happens to our nutrient requirements as we get older.

Topic 3: Dietary needs of different individuals

Babies and infants

Infants grow very quickly during the first few weeks of life so a nutritious diet is very important. All the essential nutrients can be obtained from breast milk or bottle milk formulas.

One of the Scottish dietary targets encourages breastfeeding for the first six weeks of life.

There are several advantages for the baby.

Provides all the nutrients needed by the baby.

Helps mother and baby bond.

Less expensive than bottle feeding.

Contains Omega-3 which will help brain development.

Easy to digest and more hygienic – less risk of stomach upsets.

Contains antibodies which will give protection from some illnesses.

And for the mother:

- Breastfeeding uses energy so helping the mother to lose excess fat stores gained during pregnancy.
- It is also thought that mothers who breastfeed have a lower risk of developing breast cancer.

If a baby is **bottle fed** then care must be taken to:

- Give the correct amount of infant formula to prevent over feeding, making the baby overweight.
- Prepare the bottle hygienically to reduce the risk of stomach upsets.

Weaning

Babies should not be given solid food until they are at least 4–6 months old. This is called weaning.

- Foods should contain a source of iron. Babies are born with a store of iron which will last for about 4–6 months. Iron is important for red blood cell production and to help brain development.
- Foods should not contain any added salt, sugar or additives.
- Introduce new foods gradually, with different textures and flavours to encourage a liking for a variety of foods and to alert parents to any possible allergic reactions.

✔ Test your knowledge

1. Explain two advantages of breast feeding.
2. Why is it a good idea to introduce new foods gradually to babies?

Let's Cook

Make a dish suitable for a 10-month-old, e.g. leek and potato soup or pasta in a cheesy sauce with added vegetables.

Young children

Good eating habits start in childhood, so a varied diet should be encouraged. A healthy diet will help prevent children becoming overweight.

🔑 *Key nutrients needed to unlock good health*

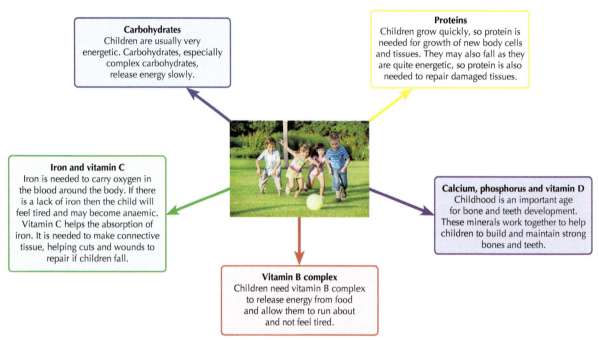

Carbohydrates
Children are usually very energetic. Carbohydrates, especially complex carbohydrates, release energy slowly.

Proteins
Children grow quickly, so protein is needed for growth of new body cells and tissues. They may also fall as they are quite energetic, so protein is also needed to repair damaged tissues.

Iron and vitamin C
Iron is needed to carry oxygen in the blood around the body. If there is a lack of iron then the child will feel tired and may become anaemic. Vitamin C helps the absorption of iron. It is needed to make connective tissue, helping cuts and wounds to repair if children fall.

Calcium, phosphorus and vitamin D
Childhood is an important age for bone and teeth development. These minerals work together to help children to build and maintain strong bones and teeth.

Vitamin B complex
Children need vitamin B complex to release energy from food and allow them to run about and not feel tired.

⚠ *Making food choices*

- Avoid giving children too many foods high in fat. Fat intake of children of primary school age should be in line with the Scottish dietary targets.

- Choose low-fat versions of dairy produce. After the age of two, semi-skimmed milk may be given, provided there is enough energy from the rest of the foods in the diet. Skimmed milk should not be given before five years of age.

- Avoid too many sugary foods, as this will contribute to obesity and tooth decay. Avoid giving sweets as a reward and avoid sugar-coated breakfast cereals.

- Encourage children to eat fruit and vegetables as low-fat and low-sugar snacks.

- Salty snacks and processed foods will encourage a liking for salt so don't have a lot of these in children's diets.

- Use food products which are additive-free.

- Include the use of naturally brightly coloured foods in meals and snacks, e.g. carrots, yellow peppers.

Make the Link

Look at the inter-relationship of nutrients in Chapter 1.

⚠ Watch point

If the question focuses on children, your answers should have a clear link to children.

☑ Test your knowledge

1. Design a breakfast suitable for a young child. Identify three different nutrients contained in the breakfast and explain why they are important to children.

2. Other than diet, explain why children may be at risk of not having enough vitamin D.

3. Explain why children should not be encouraged to develop a 'sweet tooth'.

4. List four sources of complex carbohydrates and explain how they could be included in a child's diet.

Let's Cook

Make a dessert suitable for a child, e.g. fresh fruit salad, fruit crumble, apple swiss roll, raspberry mousse.

Teenagers

The teenage years are a period of rapid growth and development. As you will have seen from the DRV charts, the need for some nutrients increases at this stage.

🔑 Key nutrients needed to unlock good health

Nutrients	Why are they needed?
Protein	Teenagers require protein for their rapid growth spurt and to repair damaged tissues, especially if a lot of sports are played.
Carbohydrates	Teenagers will need carbohydrates for energy especially if they are active. Boys may need more energy than girls because: • they tend to have a larger body size and so require more energy • they tend to be more muscular than females and so will have a greater need for energy sources to the muscles.
Calcium, phosphorus and vitamin D	The teenage years are an important time for the adult skeleton to develop, so good sources of calcium and phosphorus should be eaten to allow for strong bone development. Vitamin D is needed to help the absorption of calcium and phosphorus and so prevent osteoporosis in later life.
Iron and vitamin C	The need for iron increases as blood volume expands throughout growth, so more iron is needed to prevent tiredness and anaemia in both boys and girls. When menstruation starts, girls may need to increase their iron intake. Vitamin C helps the absorption of iron. It also helps heal cuts and wounds, especially if the teenager plays a lot of sports.
Vitamin B complex	If teenagers are active then these vitamins will help release energy from food, preventing them feeling tired.

⚠ *Making food choices*

- Many teenagers are in a rush in the morning and do not have time for breakfast. Breakfast will boost energy levels and help you concentrate on your work.
- Teenagers tend to 'graze' on snacks and fast foods which may be high in fat, sugar or salt. This increases the risk of becoming overweight, developing diabetes, heart disease in later life and cancers.
- Some teenagers spend a lot of time in front of a computer or television and are not very active, so they have to watch their energy intake so that they don't become overweight.

✔ Test your knowledge

1. **(a)** Design a packed lunch for an S1 pupil that will provide at least two macro-nutrients and three micro-nutrients.

   (b) Identify where the nutrients are found in the packed lunch and explain their importance for the pupil.

2. A teenage girl has to increase the iron and vitamin C content of her diet. List four practical ways she could do this. Explain the importance of these nutrients for health.

☕ Let's Cook

Make an energy-giving pasta dish suitable for a teenager e.g. tagliatelle bolognese, spicy chicken pasta, vegetable pasta.

Adults

During adulthood, body growth has stopped and some adults, as they become older, tend to be less active.

🔑 *Key nutrients needed to unlock good health*

Protein
To maintain and repair body cells. Remember, protein is not needed for growth in adults.

Carbohydrates
The amount of energy needed will depend on activity levels and body size. Energy should come from complex carbohydrates.

Calcium, phosphorus and vitamin D
Adulthood is an important time for bone maintenance. These nutrients help prevent osteoporosis in later life.

Iron, folic acid and vitamin C
These are needed to prevent types of anaemia. Women may develop iron deficiency anaemia due to menstruation.

⚠ *Making food choices*

- Adults who are not very active need to pay careful attention to their energy intake, especially fat intake, because if energy intake exceeds energy output then the result will be weight gain.
- Sodium (salt) intake should be reduced to help prevent high blood pressure.
- Adults should make sure they have a good range of antioxidants in their diet.
- The requirements for protein and most of the vitamins and minerals remain virtually unchanged in the adult years.

✔ Test your knowledge

1. Describe the effect on the health of adults if the energy balance is incorrect.
2. Name six sources of complex carbohydrates suitable for adults.
3. Identify the antioxidant vitamins and explain why they are important in adults' diets.

Let's Cook

Make a low-fat dish suitable for an adult.

Examples include:

- Stir-fry chicken and pineapple with rice
- Caribbean chicken with noodles

Use Quorn™ instead of chicken if you are a vegetarian.

The elderly

People are now living longer so it is important that elderly people eat a balanced diet to help them stay healthy.

🔑 *Key nutrients needed to unlock good health*

Protein

Older people may suffer more from illness and injury so will need protein to help recovery by repairing damaged cells and tissues.

Carbohydrates

Although the elderly may be less active, they still require complex carbohydrates for energy. These should include sources of fibre.

Calcium, phosphorus and vitamin D

These are important to maintain bone strength. If an elderly person does not get out a lot they may not be exposed to the sun so may lack vitamin D and be at risk of osteoporosis. They may have to take a vitamin D supplement.

Iron, folic acid and vitamin C

Missing out on these nutrients may cause anaemia.

⚠ *Making food choices*

- The elderly need smaller portions of nutritionally dense foods (foods that are good sources of several nutrients).

- An elderly person living alone may lack the motivation to prepare nutritious food and may snack on high fat and sugar foods.

- Some unsaturated fats which contain omega-3 should be included in the diet as they reduce the risk of blood clots, strokes and heart disease.

- Many elderly people tend to lose their sense of taste, so salt intake may inadvertently increase.

- A limited budget may affect food choice.

- May have difficulty chewing.

✔ Test your knowledge

1. List and explain three factors which may affect the food eaten by an elderly person.
2. Constipation is often a problem for the elderly. State three practical ways to include foods that are high in fibre in their diet.
3. Why may an elderly person be more at risk of a) osteoporosis and b) anaemia?

Let's Cook

An elderly person may not eat a lot of fruit and vegetables in their diet. Make a dish that uses these ingredients, e.g. carrot and courgette or lentil soup, fruit fool or mousse.

Women during pregnancy and lactation

The diet of a pregnant woman must meet her own nutritional needs and those of her baby. The baby will take all the nutrients first so the mother may end up deficient in some important nutrients.

Key nutrients needed to unlock good health

Nutrients	Why are they needed?
Protein	A little additional protein will be needed for the development of the unborn baby. Too much, however, could result in weight gain for the mother.
Carbohydrates	In the last three months of pregnancy the body has a greater need for energy. The baby is growing and moving around. It is important at this stage not to eat too many energy foods as too much weight can be gained, especially as the mother may not be so active. Constipation can be a problem in pregnancy. If it is, more NSP/dietary fibre should be taken, along with increased fluid intake and gentle exercise such as walking or swimming.
Iron	Providing a balanced diet is eaten, no extra iron should be needed as menstruation stops. Iron is important to provide the baby with a store of iron for the first four months after birth. It also helps the unborn baby's brain to develop.
Vitamin C	This helps iron to be absorbed, which prevents anaemia in the mother, and allows the baby to grow.
Folic acid	Women should make sure that their diet contains good supplies of folic acid before becoming pregnant and during pregnancy, especially in the first three months of pregnancy. Folic acid is needed for the development of the brain and nervous system in the foetus. This reduces the risk of babies being born with neural tube defects such as spina bifida.
Calcium, phosphorus and vitamin D	The baby's bones are supplied with calcium provided by the mother's diet. It is important that calcium intake is maintained to ensure that calcium is not taken from the mother's bones and teeth.
Unsaturated fat – omega-3	This is important during pregnancy as it helps the unborn baby's brain develop.

⚠ Food safety points

- Paté (right) and soft, ripened cheeses such as brie and camembert should not be eaten, as they may contain listeria bacteria, which can be harmful to the unborn child or result in a miscarriage. Cook/chill meals should be thoroughly reheated as they may also contain listeria bacteria.

- Eggs should be thoroughly cooked as they may contain salmonella bacteria, which can cause food poisoning. Raw egg dishes should not be eaten for the same reason.

- Pregnant women should not eat liver or liver paté as it may contain large amounts of vitamin A, which can be harmful to the unborn baby.

Make the Link

Remember the inter-relationship between iron, vitamin C and folic acid. See Chapter 1 topics.

Lactation (breastfeeding)

- A varied diet is important whilst breastfeeding to make sure that the range of nutrients needed by both mother and baby are supplied.

- Energy will be partly met from the mother's fat stores formed during pregnancy, so helping the mother lose weight.

- Breastfeeding mothers may also be advised to take a small daily supplement of vitamin D. Breast-fed babies get vitamin D from breast milk, which is why it is important for the mother to have enough for herself.

Let's Cook

Constipation can be a problem during pregnancy.

Use ingredients that are good sources of fibre to make or adapt any of the following recipes:

- Sweet and sour chicken
- Cheese and tomato pizza
- Savoury mince crumble

Test your knowledge

1. Look at RNI figures for minerals and vitamins for a woman who is breastfeeding. What are her special nutritional needs? Give examples of foods that are good sources of the nutrients she needs.

2. What could be the effect on the health of a pregnant woman if she is does not have enough calcium in her diet?

3. Explain why folic acid is important in the diet of women who want to become pregnant and during pregnancy.

4. List sources of dietary fibre/folic acid which a pregnant woman could include in her diet to prevent constipation.

Convalescents

A convalescent is someone recovering from an illness, accident or operation. The nutritional content of their diet may have to be adapted to cope with their illness.

🔑 *Key nutrients needed to unlock good health*

Calcium is needed to make up for loss of calcium from the bones as a result of a break and to help healing.

Protein is needed to allow cells and tissues damaged by illness to be repaired.

Iron is needed to make up for any blood lost as a result of an accident or operation.

Complex carbohydrates are needed as a slow release of energy but the amount required depends on the stage of recovery.

Avoid food with a *lot of fat* as the convalescent will not be as active as usual, so less energy is needed.

Vitamin C is needed to help iron to be absorbed and is essential for the immune system.

⚠ *The road to recovery*

Sugar may be required in **small** quantities to give instant energy, but take care not to have too much too often!

- Patients may need plenty of nutritious liquids, e.g. soups and broths, fruit juice, milk.

- Sources of dietary fibre such as fruit, vegetables and some wholegrain cereals will prevent constipation.

- Small portions should be served as the convalescent may have a poor appetite.

- Fatty and spicy food may cause indigestion.

- Serve colourful food to encourage appetite.

- Food should be thoroughly cooked to prevent food poisoning.

⚠ Watch point

Nutritional supplements may be added to hospital foods for patients who have difficulty eating a balanced diet.

🍵 Let's Cook

Prepare an easily digested, nutritious dish suitable for a convalescent, e.g. chicken supreme. If you can, use a computer program to analyse the suitability of the nutritional content of the dish.

☑ Test your knowledge

1. Look at the following meal served to a convalescent:
   Lentil soup, chicken casserole, boiled potatoes and broccoli.
   - Evaluate the nutritional suitability of the meal for the convalescent.

2. Using the same basic ingredients, adapt the following meal for a convalescent to make it healthier and more attractive:
   - Fried fish, cauliflower and chips followed by apple sponge pudding and custard.

Vegetarians

Vegetarian diets are used by people who, for various reasons (religious, ethnic, moral, health or personal taste), do not eat animal flesh or products. Some types of vegetarians are:

- Lacto-vegetarians, who do not eat meat, poultry, fish or eggs but will eat dairy products.

- Lacto-ovo-vegetarians, who do not eat meat, meat products, poultry or fish. They will eat animal products, dairy products and eggs.

- Ovo-vegetarians, who do not eat meat, poultry, fish or dairy products but will eat eggs.

- Vegans, who do not eat any animal or animal products.

> **⚠ Watch point**
>
> It is important to eat a well-balanced diet if you are a vegetarian to ensure the correct nutrient balance.

🗝 *Key nutrients needed to unlock good health*

Nutrients	Why are they needed?	
	Lacto-, lacto-ovo- or ovo-vegetarians	**Vegan**
Protein	The animal protein will provide the essential amino acids needed for growth and repair.	Vegetable sources of protein, e.g. pulses, cereals and nuts will provide LBV protein so a variety of sources must be combined to make up for the shortage of essential amino acids. Soya beans will provide HBV protein.
Fats	Reduced fat versions of dairy products, which would help cut down on saturated fat, should be used as an energy source.	The saturated fat content of the diet should be low as more vegetable oils are used. The omega-3 content may also be higher.
Calcium	Dairy products are good sources and will help bone strength. Ovo-vegetarians may have to use fortified food products such as flour.	Calcium can be obtained from tofu, green leafy vegetables, dried fruit, seeds and nuts. White flour and soya milks are fortified with calcium. The presence of phytic acid and fibre in wholegrain cereals may hinder the absorption of calcium.
Vitamin B12	Vitamin B12 is found in some animal products, e.g. milk, but fortified foods may have to be eaten as well.	Vegans may be at risk of developing anaemia as vitamin B12 is only found in animal foods. Supplements or fortified foods may have to be included.
Vitamin D	Found in egg yolk and margarine to assist the absorption of calcium.	Fortified foods, e.g. soya milk, may have to be eaten.
Vitamin C	Good sources must be eaten to allow the maximum amount of iron to be absorbed from food and so prevent anaemia.	
Iron	Iron may not be available to the body from certain plant foods due to phytic acid and NSP/fibre being present. The iron from vegetable sources is not so well absorbed as that from red meat. Tiredness and anaemia may result.	
Carbohydrates	Complex carbohydrates should be used as sources of energy. Wholegrain cereals, fruit and vegetables should be eaten as they provide a higher intake of dietary fibre.	

☑ Test your knowledge

1. Explain two reasons why people may become vegetarian.

2. Which vitamin may be deficient in the diet of a vegan?

3. Research the internet and any other available resources to find out the range of meat alternatives, other than Quorn™, that vegetarians can use.

« Let's Cook

Use Quorn™ chunks or mince to make a vegetarian dish. You could adapt a recipe which uses minced beef or chicken or get some ideas from www.QuornTM.co.uk/recipes/

GO! End of chapter activities

Activity 1

On your own

1 Go to www.abpischools.org.uk. Select age range 14–16, Health and Social Care, and then Balanced diet.

2 Read the information and play the Balanced diet activity, following the instructions.

Activity 2

Working in pairs: 'Sip and Crunch'

Primary 7 pupils are coming to your school for an induction day. You have been asked to develop a new drink and snack which they could have at morning interval.

These products have to be:

- Nutritionally balanced.
- 'Crunchy'. This can be provided in your drink or snack by either:
    - » The choice of ingredients, e.g. apples, peppers, carrots.
    - » The texture after cooking, e.g. baking oats in a snack.
- Appealing to primary 7 pupils.

Complete the following steps:

'Sip and Crunch' Pair Activity
Step 1 Brainstorm some possible ideas/ingredients using the information on page 63.
Step 2 Decide on your drink and snack.
Step 3 List the nutrients that will be provided by your choice of ingredients. The drink will contain the following nutrients: _____ The snack will contain the following nutrients: _____ Explain why they will be useful for primary school children: _____
Step 4 Make your 'Sip and Crunch' products.
Step 5 Carry out a simple sensory evaluation and draw a conclusion. Look at Chapter 5 for some ideas on how to present your sensory testing.

Activity 3

Working in pairs

You are going to visit Young Mums Club and as experts in nutrition you have been asked to give a presentation about the following topics:

- Good nutrition during pregnancy
- Breastfeeding advice
- Bottle feeding advice
- Weaning advice
- Feeding a toddler.

Research the key pieces of information you think you should include and produce a Powerpoint presentation for the visit.

Activity 4

Working in pairs

Very often elderly people cannot be bothered to cook. This may be due to difficulty preparing food because of lack of strength. Your class is going to come up with a series of recipes which:

- use lightweight, small electrical equipment to make food preparation easier and quicker
- are easy to cook
- contain the nutrients required by the elderly.

You and your partner will come up with one recipe. Prepare and cook the dish and make any changes to the recipe if required. Illustrate your recipe and present it in clear, easy steps. If you have grandparents or a local pensioners' club then some elderly people could try out the recipes.

Activity 5

Working in pairs: Can fast foods be part of a balanced diet?

Step 1

You and your friend enjoy fast foods but you really are not sure if they are healthy. Go to the website www.fastfoodnation.co.uk and find out some advantages and disadvantages of fast foods in the diet.

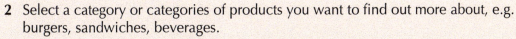

Step 2

You have both decided to treat yourself to a snack from a fast food outlet. Using www.fastfoodnutrition.org complete the following task:

1 Choose a restaurant/outlet.

2 Select a category or categories of products you want to find out more about, e.g. burgers, sandwiches, beverages.

3 Some products have the option to 'View full nutrition facts'.

You could record your results on a chart like the one below. A copy of this chart can be downloaded from www.leckieandleckie.co.uk/n45health

Restaurant/outlet chosen: _____

Food	Per serving					
	Calories/kJ	Total fat in g	Saturated fat in g	Fibre in g	Sugars in g	sodium in mg
Totals						

Step 3

Using the information about the snack you have chosen, write a conclusion about the effect it could have on the health of a teenager.

Refer to the DRV chart (e.g. the DRV for sodium is 1·6g) and GDA information (GDA for fibre is 18g) to help you.

Remember, these snacks are only part of the day's food intake.

Step 4

Make your own healthier version of a fast food burger based on the following basic recipe:

1 roll, 50g minced beef, chicken or TVP, 15ml breadcrumbs, 15ml finely chopped onion, a little egg to mix.

You may add spices to give it flavour and serve it with salad vegetables of your choice. If you have access to a nutritional computer program you could work out the nutritional value.

? Exam-style questions

To help you prepare for the exam, remember to look at pages 190–201, Keeping on track: preparing for the National 5 course assessment.

Question 1

A 16 year-old girl, who is anaemic, has the following meals in a day.

Dietary reference values for females 15–18 years					
Estimated average requirements	Reference nutrient intake				Guideline daily amounts
Energy (MJ)	Vitamin B1 (mg)	Vitamin C (mg)	Iron (mg)	Sodium (g)	Fibre (g)
8·83	0·8	40	14·8	1600	18

The table below shows the dietary analysis of a typical day's meals for the girl.

Dietary analysis of the day's meals					
Energy (MJ)	Vitamin B1 (mg)	Vitamin C (mg)	Iron (mg)	Sodium (g)	Fibre (g)
7·36	0·85	30	16·9	1800	14·2

Taking account of the Dietary Reference Values (DRVs for females aged 15–18 years) evaluate the suitability of her meals in a typical day. **6 marks**

Question 2

A parent wishes to buy a healthy snack for a toddler.

Study the information about snacks.

Nutritional information about snacks for toddlers		
Snack A	**Snack B**	**Snack C**
Energy 1·175MJ Protein 1·2g Total fat 38·0g – of which saturates 15·0g Sugar 3·58g Salt 0·45g	Energy 0·716MJ Protein 2·9g Total fat 1·1g – of which saturates 0·3g Sugar 1·5g Salt 0·17g	Energy 0.820MJ Protein 1·7g Total fat 7·8g – of which saturates 4·0g Sugar 7·2g Salt 0·21g

State the **most suitable** snack for the parent to buy for the toddler.   **1 mark**

Give **three** reasons for your choice.   **3 marks**

Now check your answers at the back of the book.

Rate your progress

How confident are you that you have achieved each of the following objectives?

Using the following key as a guide, give yourself a rating for each of the objectives below

Rating	Explanation
1	Confident with the standard of my work
2	Fairly confident with the standard of my work
3	The majority of my work was satisfactory
4	Require to do some further work
5	Require a lot of work

Objectives	Rating
Describe the benefits to health of a balanced and varied diet	
Evaluate dietary reference values with reference to specific individuals	
Explain the dietary and health needs of different individuals such as babies and infants, children, teenagers, adults, the elderly, women during pregnancy and lactation, convalescents, vegetarians	
Make food products to meet the dietary and health needs of different individuals	
Explain how food products meet the dietary and health needs of different individuals	

Look at your ratings.

Write down two **next steps** to 'unlocking' your knowledge of food and health.

4 The effects of diet-related conditions on health

After completing this chapter you should be able to:

- Explain the effect of the following diet-related conditions or diseases on health:
  - obesity
  - high blood pressure/stroke
  - heart disease
  - diabetes
  - osteoporosis, osteomalacia
  - anaemia
  - bowel disorders
  - cancers
  - dental cavities
  - food intolerances and food allergies.
- Make food products to meet dietary and health needs.
- Explain how food products meet these dietary and health needs.

Make the link

Throughout this chapter refer to Chapter 3.

Topic 1: Obesity

Obesity **may** increase the risk of developing the following diet-related diseases:

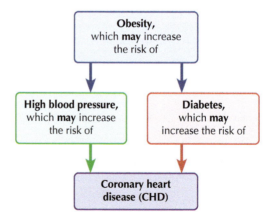

Obesity, high blood pressure (HBP) and coronary heart disease (CHD) are often linked – people may suffer from all three problems at the same time. The causes of each of these illnesses are similar.

What is obesity?

When someone becomes so overweight that the extra weight is a danger to their health, they are classed as being obese. (This is usually when they weigh about 20% or more than their ideal body weight.)

How does obesity affect health?

Increased risk of high blood pressure due to the heart being put under a lot of strain from carrying extra weight around may increase the risk of:

- strokes
- heart disease
- developing **Type 2 diabetes**
- some types of **cancer**, e.g. breast cancer
- **strain on joints**, e.g. hip, knee, which may result in wear and tear and arthritis.

How to reduce weight sensibly

The only way to reduce weight is to use up excess fat stores. This means that daily food intake must be reduced so that excess body fat is used for energy over a period of time.

Crash diets lead to a change in the metabolism (how we burn calories) and can result in the person putting on even more weight when they stop the diet.

Topic 2: High blood pressure (HBP)

How does high blood pressure (or hypertension) affect health?

Blood pressure is the pressure of blood in your arteries – these are the tubes that carry your blood from your heart to your brain and the rest of the body.

> 🔍 **Hint**
>
> High blood pressure can also be called hypertension.

What is high blood pressure?

High blood pressure is usually caused by arteries becoming narrow or damaged due to:

- Fatty deposits called **cholesterol** building up in the artery walls.
- Too much salt, which makes the heart work harder to pump the blood around the body.

How does HBP affect health?

Increased blood pressure can:

- Put a strain on the heart, which can lead to **heart disease**.

- Cause small arteries inside the brain to burst, leading to **stroke**.

Topic 3: Coronary heart disease (CHD)

What is coronary heart disease?

Heart disease results when the arteries that carry blood from the heart becomes narrowed with a gradual build up of fatty material, called cholesterol.

How does coronary heart disease affect health?

Narrowed arteries may struggle to deliver enough oxygen-rich blood to the heart. The heart is starved of oxygen, which can lead to **angina** (chest pains).

If a piece of cholesterol breaks off it may cause a blood clot to form and block the arteries.

If the blockage is close to:

- the heart, it may cause a **heart attack**,

- the brain, it may may cause a **stroke**.

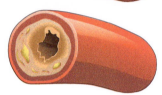

Arteries narrowing from the build up of cholesterol.

Diet-related causes	Obesity	High blood pressure	Coronary heart disease
High sugar intake Sweets and drinks with high quantities of sugar will contribute to **obesity**, **HBP** and **CHD**. Type 2 diabetes can be caused as a result of **obesity** and this increases the risk of **CHD**.	●	●	●
High total or saturated fat intake Fast foods, take-aways and snacks are popular but can be high in fat and energy content, causing **obesity** and **HBP**. **This can also cause the level of cholesterol in the blood to increase, leading to CHD.**	●	●	●
Too few polyunsaturated fats Polyunsaturated fats also reduce the risk of blood clots forming, lowering the risk of a heart attack. Omega-3, an essential fatty acid, is thought to help prevent cholesterol building up in the blood, so reducing the risk of **CHD**.			●

Diet-related causes	Obesity	High blood pressure	Coronary heart disease
High salt intake If too much salt is added to food or too many processed foods are eaten regularly then this can raise blood pressure, which can lead to **HBP** and **CHD**.		✓	✓
Diet low in fibre These types of foods are filling so people are less likely to snack on fatty foods. Fruit and vegetables are low in fat so may reduce the risk of **obesity** and lower the risk of **HBP** and **CHD**. Fibre also helps reduce the amount of cholesterol in the blood, so reducing the risk **of CHD**.	✓	✓	✓
Lack of fruit and vegetables Fruit and vegetables are good sources of antioxidant vitamins – the ACE vitamins. ACE vitamins slow down the rate at which LDL cholesterol is deposited on the artery walls, so helping to prevent **CHD**.			✓
Alcohol High alcohol intake can cause **HBP**, which may increase the risk of **CHD**. Alcohol is also high in calories, which can contribute to **obesity**.	✓	✓	✓
Causes other than diet			
Lack of regular exercise Regular exercise reduces stress, which may cause **HBP**; helps prevent **obesity**; increases stamina; strengthens the heart muscle and lowers blood cholesterol – all of which can help lower the risk of **CHD**.	✓	✓	✓
Smoking Smoking causes the blood to thicken, so increasing the risk of blood clots. Nicotine causes the heart to work faster and this increases the risk of **HBP** and **CHD**. The oxygen in the blood is reduced so the heart has to work harder, causing **HBP**.		✓	✓
Family history A family history of **HBP** or **CHD** increases the risk of developing these conditions. Some families may inherit poor eating habits in childhood that are often carried into adulthood.	✓	✓	✓
Family income Lack of money to buy food may result in a diet high in fat, sugar and salt, leading to **obesity**, **HBP** and **CHD**. Families with a higher income may eat out more, and it is often difficult to choose foods low in fat, salt and sugar when eating out.	✓	✓	✓

Diet-related causes	Obesity	High blood pressure	Coronary heart disease
Age Age increases the risk of developing **HBP** and **CHD**. Older people may be less active and eat more snack foods that are high in fat and sugar, resulting in weight gain and **obesity**.			
Lifestyle A lack of time for shopping and preparing meals may result in convenience foods and fast food meals being used – these may be high in fat, sugar and salt, causing **obesity**, **HBP** and **CHD**. Many people often 'graze' between meals on high fat, sugary foods.			

⚠ Watch point

Advertising of high fat, salt and sugar foods and promotion of special offers may encourage people to buy less healthy products, which will contibute toward obesity, HBP and CHD.

Let's Cook

Choose a dish from the recipes you have in school and adapt the ingredients to make the dish lower in fat or sugar, e.g. the sugar in scones could be reduced and dried fruit substituted; cheddar cheese could be changed to Edam cheese.

Stir-frying is considered a 'healthy' method of cooking. Using a mix of ingredients, e.g. chicken, Quorn™ or a selection of vegetables, make a stir-fry that would be suitable for someone who is trying to lose weight.

People with high blood pressure should reduce their salt intake.

Make a soup and instead of using salt add a spicy flavour, e.g. spicy lentil soup, curried butternut squash and sweet potato soup. Or use a school recipe and come up with your own flavour.

✓ Test your knowledge

1. Describe four pieces of advice you would give to a parent in order to prevent their children becoming obese.

2. Other than diet, explain two different factors which may contribute to obesity.

3. You are going to visit the local weight-watching club. Explain five pieces of advice you could give them to make sure they reduce weight sensibly.

4. Explain two health problems which could result from being overweight.

5. What is meant by 'energy balance' in the prevention of obesity?

6. Your uncle is concerned that he is at risk from coronary heart disease. Identify three dietary guidelines he should follow to reduce his risk. Explain each point.

7. Explain how smoking may contribute to CHD

8. Explain the role that omega-3 may play in CHD.

9. List and explain two pieces of advice, other than dietary, that you could give a businessman who is suffering from high blood pressure.

Topic 4: Diabetes

What is diabetes?

- During digestion food is broken down into glucose and used for energy.

- The pancreas, an organ that lies near the stomach, makes a hormone called **insulin** to help the glucose get into the cells of our bodies.

- When you have diabetes, your body either doesn't make enough insulin or can't use its own insulin as well as it should.

- This causes sugars to build up in the blood.

The two types of diabetes

Type 1 diabetes	Type 2 diabetes
The pancreas is unable to produce any insulin.	Not enough insulin is produced or the insulin that is made by the body doesn't work properly.
This type usually starts in childhood or young adulthood and is treated with insulin injections and diet control.	This type affects people as they get older but is now developing in young children, teenagers and overweight and obese people due to poor diet.
Hereditary factors play a role in the development of this type of diabetes.	This type is usually treated with a healthy diet, which includes complex carbohydrate foods.

How does diabetes affect health?

People with diabetes are more at risk of:

- Heart disease

- Strokes

- High blood pressure

- Kidney failure

- Blindness

- Circulation problems, which may result in ampuation of one or both legs.

Hint

Special diabetic products are usually more expensive and not needed if a balanced diet is eaten.

☑ Test your knowledge

Type 2 diabetes is increasing. Using resources, draw up a one-page leaflet called 'Coping with Type 2 Diabetes'. In this leaflet you should include:

- advice about diet and exercise
- an example of a recipe.

These websites will give you some information: www.diabetes.org.uk/ and www.diabetes.co.uk

🥄 Let's Cook

Smoothies could make a good start to the day for someone with diabetes. Your teacher may have some of the following or different ingredients for you and your partner to come up with an exciting new smoothie. The class could then taste and complete a sensory evaluation.

- Cucumbers
- Carrots
- Berries (raspberries, strawberries, blueberries)
- Citrus fruits (oranges, limes), bananas
- Low-fat yoghurt, reduced fat coconut milk
- Cottage cheese

Topic 5: Osteoporosis

From childhood through to the early twenties, bones develop their 'peak bone mass'. This means that they are at their maximum strength and density. From our mid 30s onwards however, we start to slowly lose calcium from our bones. This increases the risk of **osteoporosis**.

What is ostoeporosis?

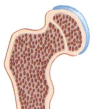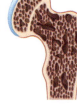

A healthy bone   The bone of an osteoporosis sufferer

- Osteoporosis means 'porous bones' and is also known as brittle bone disease.
- In osteoporosis bones lose some calcium.
- Osteomalacia results when, due to a **lack** of vitamin D, calcium or phosphorus, adults' bones become brittle.

How does osteoporosis affect health?

- Bones become thinner and weaker, which makes them more liable to break.
- Some people experience backache or notice they are getting shorter and developing a stoop due to the spine bones becoming weakened.

⚠ Watch point

Most people do not know they have osteoporosis until they have a minor fall or make an awkward movement and end up fracturing a bone. Osteoporosis develops gradually over a number of years.

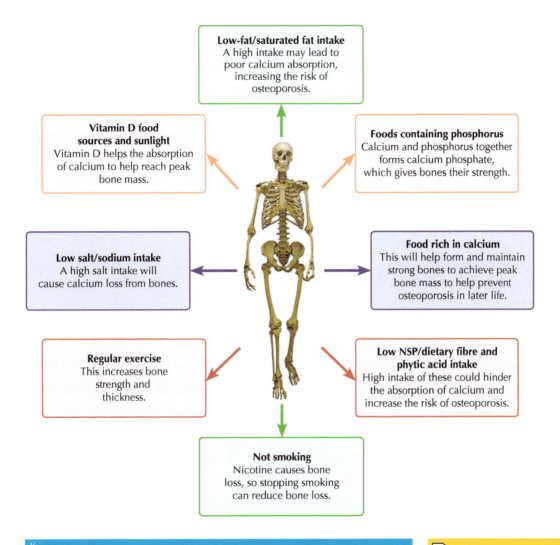

Low-fat/saturated fat intake
A high intake may lead to poor calcium absorption, increasing the risk of osteoporosis.

Vitamin D food sources and sunlight
Vitamin D helps the absorption of calcium to help reach peak bone mass.

Foods containing phosphorus
Calcium and phosphorus together forms calcium phosphate, which gives bones their strength.

Low salt/sodium intake
A high salt intake will cause calcium loss from bones.

Food rich in calcium
This will help form and maintain strong bones to achieve peak bone mass to help prevent osteoporosis in later life.

Regular exercise
This increases bone strength and thickness.

Low NSP/dietary fibre and phytic acid intake
High intake of these could hinder the absorption of calcium and increase the risk of osteoporosis.

Not smoking
Nicotine causes bone loss, so stopping smoking can reduce bone loss.

Let's Cook

People at risk of osteoporosis need good sources of calcium in their diet.

- Prepare a dish which contains ingredients rich in calcium, e.g. pane ripieno (baked filled bread) or baked bean curry. Develop some tasty new sandwich fillings using oily fish such as sardines, and some yoghurt/fromage frais-based dressings.
- You could trial your new sandwich fillings with the pupils in the class.

Test your knowledge

1. What is osteoporosis?
2. Identify and explain three causes of osteoporosis.
3. Identify foods which are rich in the nutrients needed to help reduce the risk of osteoporosis.

⚠ Watch point

Groups at risk of developing anaemia are teenagers, especially girls; pregnant women who may not have a balanced diet; the elderly; some vegetarians. Remember this if a question focuses on one of these groups.

Topic 6: Anaemia

What is anaemia?

- A shortage of iron is one cause of anaemia – iron deficiency anaemia.

- Iron forms haemoglobin (red blood cells), which causes the red colour in blood and carries oxygen to all parts of the body to be used for energy.

- If you become short of iron there will not be enough haemoglobin in the blood to carry oxygen round the body.

Causes of anaemia	How does anaemia affect health?
Not eating enough good sources of iron-rich foods, e.g. red meat, eggs, pulse vegetables, dried fruit.	You feel weak, constantly tired and short of breath.
Low intake of food rich in vitamin C to help absorption of iron.	
High intake of fibre and/or phytic acid, which prevents iron absorption.	You may have less resistance to infection and you may feel the cold more.
Less red meat may be eaten for health or personal choice reasons, e.g. vegetarians or to reduce saturated fats.	
Snacking and grazing throughout the day instead of traditional meals could mean you don't have enough iron intake.	Wounds may take longer to heal.

Let's Cook

Prepare some of the following dishes:

- Spaghetti with meatballs
- Lentil and vegetable lasagne
- Beef and broccoli stir-fry

Identify the sources of iron within the recipes.

✔ Test your knowledge

1. What is haemoglobin?
2. Describe two symptoms of iron deficiency anaemia.
3. List the groups of people most at risk from anaemia. Use chapter 3 to explain why they could be deficient in iron.
4. Describe three practical ways of including iron in the diet of a teenage girl suffering from anaemia.

Topic 7: Bowel disorders

A diet which contains high amounts of processed convenience foods which are lacking in fibre has led to an increase in the number of bowel disorders.

How do bowel disorders affect your health?

Constipation

- Constipation is usually caused by a lack of fibre and water in the diet.

- Faeces become hard and difficult to remove from the body.

Diverticular disease

- If extra strain is put on the muscular walls of the small intestine because of constipation, then diverticular disease may develop.

- If the faeces are small and hard due to a lack of fibre and water, then the muscular walls of the intestine have to work harder to move the faeces along.

- The increased pressure needed to push the waste along the intestine causes the muscular tissue to weaken and pouches to form.

- If the pouches become infected it can be very painful.

Bowel cancer

- Research has shown that a diet high in fat and red meat and low in fibre, fruit and vegetables can increase the risk of bowel cancer.

- Obesity, high alcohol intake and a lack of exercise have also been linked to bowel cancer.

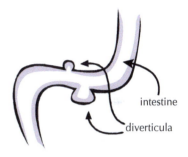

intestine

diverticula

⚠ Watch point

Diverticulitis usually only appears in people who have a diet low in NSP and are less active.

Let's Cook

Prepare dishes which contain good sources of fibre.

Some ideas are:

- vegetable and bean chilli
- tomato, lentil and lime soup
- wholemeal pastry quiche.

Or adapt one of the school recipes to include more NSP/dietary fibre.

✔ Test your knowledge

1. List at least six good sources of fibre.
2. Give three factors which can lead to bowel cancer.
3. Explain the importance of including high fibre foods in pregnant women's diets. List three dishes that include good sources of fibre.

Topic 8: Cancers

Health experts agree that eating a balanced diet could help reduce the risk of developing some cancers.

How to reduce the risk of cancers

- Eat a balanced diet which includes plenty of fruit and vegetables and moderate amounts of red and processed meats.

- Avoid becoming obese.

- Take part in regular physical activity

- Don't smoke.

- Don't drink too much alcohol.

Topic 9: Dental caries

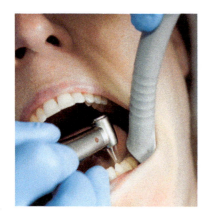

How do dental caries (tooth decay) start?

Foods that contain a high proportion of sugar are reduced to a very sticky film when they are chewed and mixed with saliva. Even after swallowing, sugary particles called plaque are left sticking to the teeth.

Bacteria which are normally present in the mouth attack the plaque and change it to acid. The acid gradually eats away at the enamel on the teeth and decay will start.

Sugars found naturally in foods (intrinsic sugars), e.g. fruit, have a less harmful effect on the teeth. Extrinsic sugars such as sucrose (table sugar), found in sweets, soft drinks and cakes causes the most tooth decay.

Preventing tooth decay

Cause of tooth decay	Practical ways of preventing tooth decay
High sugar intake	Cut down on sugary food and drinks, especially between meals, as the sugar stays on the teeth. Read food labels, as many foods contain 'hidden sugar'.
Not enough calcium, phosphorous and vitamin D	Good food sources must be eaten to give teeth their hardness.
Not enough vitamin C	Foods that contain vitamin C will help keep gums healthy.
Eating too much salt/sodium	Eating too much could lead to a loss of calcium, so weakening the teeth.

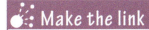

Regularly drinking diet drinks will cause tooth decay due to their acidity. Crunchy foods such as carrots, celery and apples should be eaten to exercise the gums and help prevent infection.

Make the link

Look at Chapter 1: Inter-relationship of nutrients.

✔ Test your knowledge

1. Good oral hygiene is also important in preventing dental caries. Explain five ways of implementing good oral hygiene.
2. Explain three other ways, which are not included in the chart above, to reduce sugar intake in the diet.
3. State four points of advice you would give a mother of a two-year-old toddler to help prevent the child developing tooth decay.

Let's Cook

Prepare coleslaw using crunchy ingredients such as apples, carrots, cabbage and celery, or develop a calcium-rich dip to serve with some crunchy vegetable sticks.

Topic 10: Food intolerance and food allergies

For some people, eating certain foods can cause bad reactions.

Food intolerences

Food intolerance is the general term used to describe when the body reacts badly to a certain food or ingredient. It also includes foods that cause allergic reactions. Examples are:

i. Lactose intolerance

What is a lactose intolerance?	How is health affected?	What can help?
People with lactose intolerance cannot digest the milk sugar called **lactose**.	They may suffer from cramps, feeling sick, swollen abdomen and diarrhoea after drinking cow's milk.	Using products made from soya milk and other lactose-free products.

ii. Gluten intolerance (coeliac disease)

What is gluten intolerance?	How is health affected?	What can help?
People who are sensitive to **gluten**, the protein substance found in wheat, rye, oats and barley food products, develop **coeliac disease**.	The lining of the intestine is damaged by the gluten and this prevents nutrients being absorbed. Children don't grow properly and adults often have anaemia, weight loss and diarrhoea.	There is a large range of gluten-free products available in supermarkets. When you see the crossed grain symbol on packaging it tells you that food is gluten-free.

Food allergies

What is a food allergy?	Which foods cause allergies?	How is health affected?
Food allergies happen when the body's immune system reacts strongly to a particular substance.	Allergies to soya, peanuts, shellfish and eggs are the most common but there are an increasing number of other foods.	**Mild** reaction can include headaches, asthma, skin irritations and sickness and diarrhoea.
	Some food colours and preservatives cause hyperactivity in children.	**Severe** reaction can cause breathing difficulties and lead to **anaphylactic shock**. This can happen to some people within seconds of eating, for example, peanuts or shellfish and can be fatal.

⚠ Watch point

Sometimes small amounts of an allergen can get into a product by accident, even though food producers take great care to stop this happening. If there is a possibility that this could happen in a factory, the food label might say something such as 'may contain nuts'.

Clear food labelling is very important for people who have severe allergic reactions to some foods. Some people have to carry an epipen for severe allergic reactions.

Since November 2005 European Union (EU) legislation has stated that the following 14 allergen (allergy-causing) ingredients have to be shown on pre-packed foods sold within the EU:

Cereals containing gluten (wheat, barley, rye and oats) celery, shellfish (prawns, lobster and crab), eggs, fish, lupin (flour or seeds), milk, molluscs (mussels, oysters), mustard, nuts, e.g. hazelnut, almonds, walnuts, Brazil nuts, cashew and pecan, peanuts, sesame seeds, soya beans and soya products, sulphur dioxide and sulphites (preservatives used in food and drinks).

🍵 Let's Cook

Your aunt has coeliac disease. She enjoys a baked treat with her cup of tea. Look up some gluten free recipes, e.g. http://www.channel4. com/4food/recipes/special-diet/ gluten-free/chocolate-muffins-recipe. You could work in pairs and make another batch using ordinary flour. Then you could compare the result.

☑ Test your knowledge

Visit www.nutrition.org.uk. Select Nutrition Science, Food Allergy and Intolence. Choose either wheat intorerence or peanut allergy. Read the information.

For the diet condition you choose, give four points of advice which should be followed.

GO! End of chapter activities

Activity 1

On your own

Make up a crossword on dietary diseases using the information in this chapter. Go to www.eclipsecrossword.com and follow the instructions.

You could use this activity to help you build a bank of crosswords that could be used to revise any of the topics in the Health and Food Technology course. You could test your friends by getting them to complete your crossword.

Activity 2

On your own

Go to www.foodafactoflife.org.uk. Select 11–16, Diet and Health. Complete the following interactive activities:

- Diet through life
- Tips for healthy eating
- Obesity.

Activity 3

In groups

'Dietary diseases – the bigger picture'

The teacher will tell you which of the following dietary diseases your group is going to investigate. Each group will have to produce a wall chart with information about **one** of the following:

- Coronary heart disease
- Anaemia
- Osteoporosis
- High blood pressure
- Obesity.

Step 1

In your group, brainstorm on a piece of paper what you are going to include in the wall chart under each of the following headings:

- Causes
- Effect on health
- Prevention
- Possible groups of people at risk
- Key points of advice to prevent this dietary disease
- Recipe suggestions.

Step 2

Build your wall chart.

Collect any interesting newspaper, magazine or web articles, or news clips about the dietary disease to use for your wall chart.

Step 3

Your task now is to become the 'experts' on this dietary disease. Decide on a way to share your expertise with the rest of the class.

Step 4

After completing the group task do the following work **on your own**.

a. Identify at least three diet-related diseases.

b. Explain at least one effect on health of each diet-related disease you have identified.

Do this task well, as it could be kept for your portfolio of work.

> Do this task well if you are working on your own, as it could be kept for your portfolio of work.

Activity 4

Working on your own, in pairs or in a small group.

Carry out one or more of the following activities.

Case study A

Ian is in third year at secondary school and wants to play in the school football team. Lately he has felt very tired and his doctor has told him that he is anaemic.

- Identify possible reasons for his anaemia.
- Outline the dietary advice you would give to Ian.
- Select and prepare a dish suitable for an evening meal to help him meet his needs.
- Explain how the dish meets Ian's dietary and health needs.

Case study B

Susan has gained a lot of weight whilst on holiday due to her 'sweet tooth'.

- Explain any dietary and health advice you could give Susan to help her lose weight.
- Select and prepare a dessert that would help Susan lose the weight she has gained.
- Explain how the dish meets Susan's dietary and health needs.

Case study C

Anne's grandmother has developed osteoporosis. Although Anne is only 15 years old, she is aware that the teenage years are an important time for bone development.

- Explain any dietary and health advice you could give to Anne to help reduce the risk of osteoporosis in her own future.
- Select and prepare a dish which would contribute to lowering this risk.
- Explain how the dish meets Anne's dietary and health needs.

Case study D

There is a history of high blood pressure in Marie's family, so she is keen to reduce the risk of developing high blood pressure later on in life.

- Explain any dietary and health advice you could give to Marie to reduce the risk of high blood pressure later on in her life.
- Select and prepare a dish that would help reduce this risk.
- Explain how the dish meets Marie's dietary and health needs.

Case study E

Sam, who has just started training as an accountant, has been told by the doctor that he is suffering from diverticulitis.

- Explain any dietary and health advice you could give to Sam to help him cope with diverticulitis.
- Select and prepare a lunchtime snack that would help reduce the discomfort of the condition.
- Explain how the dish meets Sam's dietary and health needs.

Activity 4 proforma: Complete the following proforma

A copy of the proforma can be downloaded from www.leckieandleckie.co.uk/n45health

Case study _____

Step 1: Advice

The key factors you will have to consider linked to the case study are:

- Dietary and health advice linked to the dietary disease/condition.
- Suitable ingredients/cooking methods that could be used in a dish for the person.
- Select a suitable dish.

Step 2

Complete a food order for your selected dish.
Dish chosen _____

Ingredient	Quantity	Ingredient	Quantity

Step 3

Prepare the dish.

Step 4

- Explain how the dish meets or does not meet the dietary and health needs of the person in the case study.
- Explain any changes or improvements you might make to your dish.

? Exam-style questions

To help you prepare for an exam, remember to look at pages 191–202, Keeping on track: preparing for the National 5 course assessment.

Question 1

State **two** ways of avoiding **each** of the following:

a) High blood pressure

b) Osteoporosis   **4 marks**

Question 2

i.   Describe **two** factors which may contribute to obesity.   **2 marks**

ii. Name **two** dietary diseases linked to obesity.   **2 marks**

Question 3

Identify and explain **two** factors which may contribute to coronary heart disease.   **4 marks**

Question 4

A 54-year-old call centre worker who has high blood pressure wishes to improve her diet.

Dietary reference values for females 50+ years					
Estimated average requirements	Reference nutrient intake				Guideline daily amounts
Energy (MJ)	Protein (mg)	Vitamin B1 (mg)	Iron (mg)	Sodium (g)	Fibre (g)
8·0	46·5	0·8	8·7	1·6	18

The table below shows the dietary analysis of a typical day's menu for this female.

Dietary analysis of the day's meals					
Energy (MJ)	Protein(mg)	Vitamin B1 (mg)	Iron (mg)	Sodium (g)	Fibre (g)
11·20	48·0	1·2	4·8	2·1	12

Taking account of the Dietary Reference Values (DRVs) for females aged 50+, evaluate the suitability of her typical day's meals.   **6 marks**

Now check your answers at the back of the book.

Rate your progress

How confident are you that you have achieved each of the following objectives?

Using the following key as a guide, give yourself a rating for each of the objectives below

Rating	Explanation
1	Confident with the standard of my work
2	Fairly confident with the standard of my work
3	The majority of my work was satisfactory
4	Require to do some further work
5	Require a lot of work

Objectives	Rating
Explain the effect of the following diet-related conditions or diseases on health:	
• Obesity	
• High blood pressure/strokes	
• Heart disease	
• Diabetes	
• Osteoporosis	
• Anaemia	
• Bowel disorders	
• Cancers	
• Dental caries	
• Food intolerances and food allergies	
Make food products to meet dietary and health needs	
Explain how food products meet these dietary and health needs	

Look at your ratings.

Write down two **next steps** to 'unlocking' your knowledge of food and health.

This unit will develop knowledge and understanding of the functional properties of ingredients in food and their use in developing new food products. You will learn about the stages involved in developing food products and will use this knowledge to produce food products for specified needs, safely and hygienically.

By the end of this unit you should be able to:

OUTCOME 1: EXPLAIN HOW FOOD PRODUCTS ARE DEVELOPED.

This means you have to:

- Explain the functional properties of different ingredients in food products.
- Explain the stages of food product development.

OUTCOME 2: DEVELOP A FOOD PRODUCT TO MEET SPECIFIED NEEDS.

This means you have to:

- Undertake investigations to generate ideas for food products that meet specified needs.
- Make a prototype of a food product using safe and hygienic practices.
- Conduct a sensory evaluation of the food product.
- Explain how the food product meets the specified needs.

2

Food Product
Development

5 The functional properties of different ingredients in food products

After completing this chapter you should be able to:

- Explain the functional properties of the following ingredients in food products:
  - eggs
  - flour
  - sugar
  - fat
  - milk/liquid.
- Make food products which demonstrate these functional properties.
- Explain the effects on the finished product of changing the proportions of ingredients.

What does 'functional properties' mean?

When manufacturers design food products, the ingredients are chosen for their **properties** or **function** in the recipe as well as their nutritional qualities.

What happens to food during processing depends on these properties. To make successful products, food technologists use these properties, which are described as **functional properties**.

Topic 1: The functional properties of eggs

Aeration

How it works	What is it used for?
When egg white is beaten it traps air and forms a foam, making sponges lighter. This is due to the protein in the egg stretching and trapping air bubbles to make foam. When egg is whisked with sugar, a large volume of air is trapped in a honeycomb-like mesh. Eggs hold air in cakes and act as a raising agent. ⚠ If the egg white is not beaten enough the foam will not have a good volume. If it is over-beaten the protein in the egg is overstretched and the foam collapses. Eggs give a better volume when whisked at room temperature.	Meringues; swiss roll; whisked sponges.

Emulsifying

How it works	What is it used for?
Egg yolk contains a substance which acts as an emulsifier. This is used to prevent mixtures of oil and other liquids, e.g. vinegar, from separating. In cake-making the egg yolk forms an emulsion with the fat and oil in the margarine and the liquid in the egg. This prevents the fat from separating from the liquid (the sugar and eggs), which would cause the mixture to separate out or curdle. ⚠ Eggs should be at room temperature and added gradually when making an emulsion in cake-making, to prevent curdling.	Mayonnaise; cake-making. 

Coagulation

How it works	What is it used for?
When eggs are heated they change from a fluid state to a more solid state. This is called coagulation. Coagulation thickens fillings and quiches. When eggs are mixed into a liquid, e.g. milk, and then heated, coagulation makes the mixture thicken. Egg white thickens or sets between 60°C and 65°C. Egg yolk thickens at 65°C and eventually thickens at 70°C. ⚠ If egg proteins are heated too long or at too high a temperature then the result is a hard and tough mass. This is easily seen when eggs are overcooked, e.g. scrambled eggs become tough and liquid appears because the proteins within the egg shrink and the liquid is squeezed out.	Egg custard; bread and butter pudding; quiche. 

Binding

How it works	What is it used for?
The egg proteins coagulate when heated and bind or hold combinations of ingredients together. ⚠ When cooking, the heat should be at the right temperature so that the egg coagulates and holds the ingredients together to produce an unbroken product.	Fishcakes; hamburgers; rissoles, biscuits. 
Eggs can also give a golden brown colour and add more flavour to products.	Pastry, scones.

⁝∴ Make the Link

Topic 5 in this chapter will give you more information on the effect of eggs on finished products.

Topic 2: The functional properties of flour

Both the starch and gluten contained in flour have an effect on the finished product. Gluten is the stretchy protein substance found in flour.

Gelatinisation

How it works	What is it used for?
In sauce making, when starch and water are heated, the water is absorbed through the walls of the starch granules, which then swell and burst. This thickens the liquid and is called gelatinisation. Gelatinisation allows a sauce to set when cooled, e.g. custard powder made from cornflour thickens when heated with milk and when cold it sets and can be used for trifles. ⚠ If the gelatinisation process does not take place properly in sauce making it could result in: • the sauce being lumpy if it has not been stirred all the time or heated too quickly • the sauce being too thin if it has not been brought to the boil.	Sauces, soups. 

Fermentation

How it works	What is it used for?
Fermentation results when yeast, under the right conditions, produces carbon dioxide and alcohol – this allows flavour, texture and volume to develop, e.g. bread-making. In bread-making, this takes place during the time that the dough is set aside to prove (rise). Strong flour is the most suitable for bread-making as it has a high gluten content, which gives a stretchy and elastic dough. When the dough is cooked, steam is produced by the liquid, the gluten is stretched by the bubbles of CO_2 gas produced from the yeast and the bread rises and sets. ⚠ The type of flour used will affect the finished product in different ways. • Wholemeal flour adds a nutty flavour and crunchy texture to baked products. • Wholemeal flour contains more B complex vitamins and fibre, making the product more nutritious.	Bread or other yeast-based products. 

> ## ⚠ Watch point
>
> To obtain successful results the conditions for fermentation must be correct. These are:
>
> - the correct amount of yeast
> - a source of food (sugar or flour)
> - moisture
> - the correct temperature – fermentation works best at 25°C–29°C and stops at 55°C, when the yeast is killed.
>
> If the bread is left too long to ferment the gluten becomes overstretched and loses elasticity. The food product is heavy and not well risen. If the bread has not had enough time to ferment, then not enough CO_2 gas forms and the gluten does not stretch enough. The finished bread has a heavy, close texture.

Dextrinisation

How it works	What is it used for?
The surface starch in scones, pastry or cakes changes to dextrin during the cooking time in the dry heat of the oven. This helps baked goods to become a golden brown colour. Toast also browns by dextrinisation. ⚠ If over-cooked the product will become burnt, so check the temperature and the time!	Bread, cakes, biscuits. Toast. 

✔ Test your knowledge

1. Explain what happens during gelatinisation.
2. List three products which use the functional property of gelatinisation.
3. Describe what happens during the fermentation process in bread making.
4. State two products which use the functional property of dextrinisation.

🍲 Let's Cook

Make a product using flour to show some of the following functional properties:

- Gelatinisation: cauliflower and cheese sauce.
- Fermentation: packet bread mix to make rolls.

Topic 3: The functional properties of sugar

Crystallisation

How it works	What is it used for?
Sugar dissolves in water. When sugar (sucrose) and water are boiled, the water is driven off, the concentration becomes greater and eventually a thick sticky syrup is formed. This sets into very fine crystals on cooling. The amount of sugar used must be correct – too much will cause large crystals to form. The sugar mixture should not be stirred while the sugar is dissolving or boiling – if the mixture is disturbed by stirring, then crystals will start to form on the surface of the spoon and a crunchy mixture with large crystals may result. Sugar prevents food spoilage in jams because it acts as a preservative.	Manufacturers make use of this property during jam-making, boiled sweets, tablet and toffee-making. 

Caramelisation

How it works	What is it used for?
Sugar helps to colour products, such as the top of cakes, by caramelising in the heat of the oven. When sugar is heated in a liquid or when used as a topping, it begins to caramelise and turn brown due to the heat.  ⚠ If heated too long sugar becomes black in appearance and has a bitter flavour.	Cakes. Tablet, toffee. Sugar can also be sprinkled on the top of crème caramel and browned under a hot grill or with a cook's blowtorch. This gives a toffee flavour and adds crunch.

> ### ⚫⚬ Make the Link
>
> Topic 6 in this chapter will give you more information on the effect of different proportions of sugar on the finished product.

Aeration and flavour

How it works	What is it used for?
Aeration Sugar also traps air when it is creamed with fat, making the end result lighter in texture. It also helps the yeast to rise in bread-making. **Flavour** Sugar makes foods sweeter.	Cake making, all types of bread. Desserts, cakes and biscuits.

✔ Test your knowledge

1. Explain what happens to sugar when it is heated in water.

2. State two ways in which a manufacturer can use the property of crystallisation.

3. Explain why the sugar mixture should not be stirred while the sugar is dissolving.

4. Explain what happens during caramelisation.

🍴 Let's Cook

Make a product using sugar to show some of the following functional properties:

- Crystallisation: jam, toffee apples
- Caramelisation: summer fruit brulee

Topic 4: The functional properties of fat

Aeration: creaming

How it works		What is it used for?
Fat and caster sugar are beaten or creamed together until they form a foam. Air is trapped in the mixture in tiny bubbles, which makes the mixture lighter and helps the cake to rise. ⚠ Creaming is easier when the fat is at room temperature or a soft margarine is used.		Cakes, biscuits. 

Aeration: rubbing in

How it works		What is it used for?
Fat is rubbed into the flour and coats the flour particles. The mixture should look like breadcrumbs. This forms a waterproof barrier but also traps air as the mixture is lifted and rubbed in with the fingertips. Keep the fat and fingertips as cool as possible when rubbing in to prevent the mixture becoming oily.		Pastry, cakes, biscuits. 

Shortening

How it works	What is it used for?
Fats have a 'shortening' effect. This gives the mixture a crumbly, 'short' texture. This texture is created by the fat coating the flour particles. Some flour particles remain uncoated when fat is rubbed in. When water is added to shortcrust pastry, the uncoated flour particles absorb the water and for this type of pastry the less water added, the 'shorter' the pastry, with a 'melt in the mouth' texture. ⚠ A fat that coats the flour particles easily will give the best results. Liquid oils can also be used to shorten mixtures because they coat the flour particles thoroughly and give a crumbly product.	Pastry, shortbread and biscuit mixtures. 

Flavour and colour

How it works	What is it used for?
The type of fat used will affect the flavour and colour, e.g. butter gives a richer taste and using a white fat will give a paler colour.	Shortbread, pastry.

 Make the Link

Topic 6 in this chapter will give you more information on the effect of different proportions of fat on the finished product.

Keeping qualities

How it works	What is it used for?
Fat is used to improve the keeping qualities of foods, i.e. the length of time a food is edible.	Victoria sandwich.

 Let's Cook

Make a product using fat to show some of the following functional properties:

- Aeration: cup cakes
- Shortening: shortbread.

☑ **Test your knowledge**

1. Explain how the property of 'shortening' is used in making pastry.

2. Describe how air is added during **a)** creaming and **b)** rubbing in.

3. Why should your fingertips be cool when rubbing fat into flour?

Topic 5: The functional properties of liquid (water, milk, egg)

Functional property	How it works	What is it used for?
Aeration	Liquid helps cake mixtures to rise by producing steam in the heat of the oven and is also needed by raising agents to help them work. The yeast in bread making also needs liquid to allow it to grow and multiply.	Cakes, biscuits, bread
Gelatinisation	During baking and sauce-making liquid is needed for gelatinisation with the starch to take place.	Cakes, sweet and savoury sauces
Nutritional value	Using egg and milk in a product will add extra nutrients to the dish.	Mashed potatoes, custards and sauces
Colour and flavour	Egg will give a richer colour to dishes and improves the flavour.	Rice pudding, egg glaze

☑ Test your knowledge

1. Describe how liquid will help a cake to rise in the oven.

2. State two products where each of the following functional properties of liquid could be used to improve the end results:

   a) the colour

   b) flavour

   c) the nutritional value.

Make the Link

Topic 6 in this chapter will give you more information on the effect of different proportions of liquid on the finished product.

Let's Cook

Make a batch of scones using different liquids to show the functional property colour. Use the following ingredients:

1. Egg as the liquid and the glaze.

2. Milk as the liquid and the glaze.

3. Egg and milk as the liquid and the glaze.

Compare the results.

Topic 6: Factors that affect finished products

The proportion of ingredients used

It is important to weigh and measure ingredients correctly, as the end product can be affected by the slightest variations.

Sugar

Decreasing sugar in a product:
- gives less flavour
- gives poorer keeping qualities
- gives a paler colour
- prevents cakes from rising.

Increasing sugar in a product:
- results in a longer cooking time, which gives a darker colour
- gives some foods a sugary, crunchy texture
- produces very soft mixtures during baking, which then become hard when cool
- gives a sweeter result
- can result in cake sinking in the middle as the gluten has been over-softened so that it collapses
- can result in fruit sinking in a fruit cake as the structure will collapse.

Fat

Reducing fat in a product results in:
- baked items not keeping so well and becoming stale more quickly
- less flavour in scones and cakes
- a paler colour
- the texture of scones and cakes not being so soft and moist
- pastry being hard and tough.

Increasing fat in a product results in:
- a greasy flavour and texture in cakes and pastry
- a richer flavour
- a darker colour
- pastry being very crumbly and easily broken.

Liquid

Not adding **enough liquid** can result in:
- scones, bread having a heavy texture and not rising very quickly or well
- cakes having a dry texture
- shortcrust pastry being easily broken and crumbly.

Adding **too much liquid** can result in:
- dough being sticky to handle
- bread having a coarse and open texture
- scone dough being too soft and spreading, so losing shape during cooking
- cakes having a heavy, doughy texture and the top may be cracked
- fruit sinking in a fruit cake if the mixture is too wet
- hard and tough shortcrust pastry.

Cooking time and temperature

Colour of the finished product can be controlled by the **temperature** and length of **time** it is cooked, e.g. a cake baked at a low temperature or for a short time will be paler than one baked at a higher temperature or for a longer time.

Colour can also be affected by the **cooking method** used. When food is grilled or baked it turns brown due to dextrinisation or caramelisation. The colour changes very little when food is microwaved or steamed.

Make the Link

The activities for this chapter will give you an opportunity to trial and taste products made using different proportions of ingredients.

✔ Test your knowledge

1. Describe two effects of increasing sugar in a baked product.

2. Identify and discuss two effects that the proportion of fat may have on a product.

3. State the effect on the following:

   a) Scones which have had too much liquid added.

   b) Pastry which has had too little water added.

   c) A fruit cake that has had too much liquid added.

🍲 Let's Cook

Make shortcrust pastry using:

- Different types of flour – wholemeal, white, and a mixture of wholemeal and white flours.

- Different types of fats – butter, margarine, white fat and a mixture of margarine and white fat.

Make each batch of pastry into individual tartlet cases and bake blind.

Comment on the effect of the changes with regard to colour, texture and flavour.

Fill the preferred tartlet cases with a yoghurt, cream and fruit mix to make individual fruit tartlets.

GO! End of chapter activities

Activity 1

On your own

Choose one of the following food products.

- Quiche Lorraine
- Whisked sponge

    a) Select at least three ingredients which are used in the product.

    b) Describe at least one functional property of each of the three selected ingredients.

    c) Explain how each of the functional properties will affect the finished product.

Do this task well as it could be kept for your portfolio of work.

Activity 2

Working in groups or as a class

Investigate the effect of different proportions of ingredients in cake making.

Step 1

Make a sponge using the following recipe – this will be the control.

Basic recipe	Method
50g SR flour 50g margarine 50g caster sugar 1 egg 15ml water.	1. Grease and line a 15cm sandwich tin. Put on oven gas mark 5, 190°C. 2. Place all ingredients into a bowl and beat together until smooth. 3. Place into the lined and greased tin. 4. Bake for 20–25 minutes. 5. Cool.

Step 2

Prepare the other sponges using the same method but with the following changes:

a) 100g margarine, 50g caster sugar, 50g SR flour, 1 egg, 15ml water.

b) 10g margarine, 50g caster sugar, 50g SR flour, 1 egg, 15ml water.

c) 100g sugar, 50g margarine, 50g SR flour, 1 egg, 15ml water.

d) 10g sugar, 50g margarine, 50g SR flour, 1 egg, 15ml water.

e) 50g caster sugar, 50g margarine, 75g SR flour, 1 egg, 15ml water.

f) 50g caster sugar, 50g margarine, 25g SR flour, 1 egg, 15ml water.

g) No egg, 50g caster sugar, 50g margarine, 50g SR flour, 15ml water.

h) 50g caster sugar, 50g margarine, 50g SR flour and 25g wholemeal SR flour, 1 egg, 15ml water.

Step 3

Complete the following table using a rating system. 1 = very good, 2 = good, 3 = satisfactory, 4 = not good 5 = very bad. The tables below can be downloaded from www.leckieandleckie.co.uk/n45health

Results				
Sample	Colour	Appearance	Texture	Taste
Control				
a) 100g fat increasing fat				
b) 10g fat reducing fat				
c) 100g sugar increasing sugar				
d) 10g sugar decreasing sugar				
e) 75g flour increasing flour				
f) 25g SR flour decreasing flour				
g) No egg				
h) 50g SR flour and 25g SR wholemeal flour				

Step 4: Conclusion

What are the properties of the following ingredients and how did changing the proportions affect the finished result?

Ingredient	Functional properties	Effect on finished result
Margarine		
Caster sugar		
Flour		

Activity 3

On your own

Produce a flow diagram to show the process of gelatinisation of starch granules.

Activity 4

Eggs can be used in a variety of ways. The local supermarket wishes to promote the sale of eggs at Easter time at an 'Eggstravaganza'.

Either:

* Design and make a range of products to promote their versatility *or*
* Produce a poster which could be displayed at the supermarket showing their use.

❓Exam-style questions

To help you prepare for the exam, remember to look at pages 191–202, Keeping on track: preparing for the National 5 course assessment.

Question 1

The in-store bakery of a supermarket is developing a new range of cakes. The results of product-testing are as follows:

	Result
Cake A	Has sunk in the middle.
Cake B	Cherries have sunk to the bottom.
Cake C	Heavy, doughy texture

Give a **different** reason why each result may have happened.   **3 marks**

Question 2

Give **one** function of **each** of the following ingredients in a baked product.

- Eggs
- Sugar   **2 marks**

Question 3

Describe how changing the proportion of ingredients in **each** of the following products could affect the finished result.

a) Increase the proportion of flour in a sauce.

b) Increase the proportion of sugar in a sponge.

c) Increase the proportion of fat in pastry.   **3 marks**

Question 4

a) Describe **two** uses of fat in a product.   **2 marks**

b) Apart from sweetness, describe **two** uses of sugar in a product.   **2 marks**

Now check your answers at the back of the book.

Rate your progress

How confident are you that you have achieved each of the following objectives?

Using the following key as a guide, give yourself a rating for each of the objectives below

Rating	Explanation
1	Confident with the standard of my work
2	Fairly confident with the standard of my work
3	The majority of my work was satisfactory
4	Require to do some further work
5	Require a lot of work

Objectives	Rating
Explain the functional properties of the following ingredients in food products:	
• Eggs	
• Flour	
• Sugar	
• Fat	
Make food products which demonstrate these functional properties	
Explain the effects on the finished product of changing the proportions of ingredients	

Look at your ratings.

Write down two **next steps** to 'unlocking' your knowledge of food product development.

6 The stages of food product development

After completing this chapter you should be able to:

- Explain the stages of food product development.
- Undertake investigations to generate ideas for food products that meet specified needs.
- Make a prototype of a food product using safe and hygienic practices.
- Conduct sensory evaluations of food products.
- Explain how a food product meets specified needs.

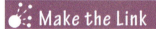 **Make the Link**

Throughout this chapter refer to Chapter 7.

Topic 1: The stages of food product development

Food product development – unravel the many stages

Manufacturers are constantly having to develop and update their products to keep up with the demands of a continually changing society, developments in technology, changing retail food outlets and the buying power of the consumer.

The development of any new product is a costly process, therefore food manufacturers have to come up with a food development strategy to help them get it right.

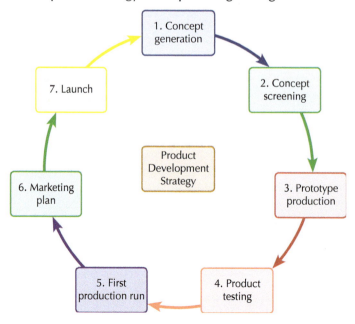

Step 1: Concept generation – 'The thinking stage'

- Development of new ideas.

- Identifying any gaps in the market.

- Using market analysis to trial existing products to find out what makes them popular.

- Identifying changes that could be made to existing products.

- Cost, portion size, flavour, appearance, texture, and preparation are all considered at this point.

> Without this stage the development strategy cannot go forward.

Step 2: Concept screening – 'Time to consider those ideas'

- Analysis of all the ideas from the thinking stage and prioritising them.

- Developing a specification.

- Discarding any of the ideas that might be costly, difficult to process or do not meet all the requirements of the specification.

- Taking forward the best ideas to the next stage.

> This stage is important to allow the production process to move away from the initial ideas to actual development possibilities.

Step 3: Prototype production – 'Time to make samples of a possible product'

- Making up examples or specimens of what the product will look like.

- Ensuring the product will meet the needs of the target group.

- Make any changes, if required, to the prototype.

> There may be more than one prototype at this stage.

Step 4: Product testing – 'Trial the initial ideas'

- Trialling the prototypes with a range of consumers through the use of tasting panels etc. aimed at specific groups such as workforces, social groups, age groups.

- Using the opinions gained to either eliminate or make refinements to the product.

> This stage is important as it allows the product to be tested on consumers and opinions used to move the product on to the next stage.

Step 5: First production run – 'Time to test the product with the consumers'

- The new product is produced for the first time as a full production run so the item can be assessed.

- Quality-assurance team tests the production run for quality and standard of the product.

> This is an important stage as any changes that need to be made will affect some of the previous stages in the development of the product, e.g. if ingredients are changed.

Step 6: Marketing plan – 'Time to get ready to launch the product'

- An advertising campaign is developed to promote the product.

- Decisions made on where the product will be sold, e.g. supermarket, corner shop.

- Promotional activities decided, e.g. where it is to be positioned in the shop, free recipe cards, money-off vouchers.

- Packaging finalised and selling price agreed.

> This is an important stage as the initial price of the product can be determined by the potential marketing mix, e.g. low cost to attract interest (e.g. shop's own brand); medium/ high cost to denote quality (luxury ranges).

Step 7: Product launch – 'Time to get it on the shelves!'

- This is an important stage as the product is now on sale.

- Market monitoring – the product is finally launched into the national marketplace and sales figures are checked very carefully.

> A range of promotional techniques need to be used to help promote the sales of the product, e.g. in-store tasting, special offers, TV adverts.

Disassembly and the manufacturer

What is disassembly?
To disassemble means to take something apart.

Who uses disassembly and why?
Manufacturers and Trading Standards officers.

Manufacturers use disassembly to:

- Assess an existing product, especially if there has been a drop in sales or they wish to produce a new or improved version of it.

- Ensure quality and that the product remains at its best during storage, purchase and use.

- Find out more information about how a food product has been designed.

- Investigate how the proportion and variety of ingredients will affect the cost and nutritional value of the product.

Trading Standards Officers use disassembly to:

- Check that manufacturers are meeting legal requirements and packaging claims.

How is disassembly done?

Stage 1
A chart or form should be designed before you start. This should list the procedures to be carried out and the questions that have to be answered. The form will vary depending on what has to be found out. It may include the following:
- Sensory characteristics such as taste, texture, appearance and aroma
- Choice and suitability of ingredients
- Proportions of ingredients
- Preparation and cookery processes used
- Quality of product
- Storage and shelf-life
- Value for money
- Overall evaluation of product.

Stage 2
Disassemble the product by starting with the information on the label and the shape/size of the package.

Stage 3
Take the food product apart and weigh and measure the different parts of the product. For example if a sandwich is disassembled, the bread, spread and each item of filling need to be weighed separately.

Stage 4
Compare the results from each product disassembled.

⚠ **Watch point**

Using a form ensures that the same method of analysis is used for every sample so that 'like can be compared with like' in the evaluation.

What can disassembly tell us?

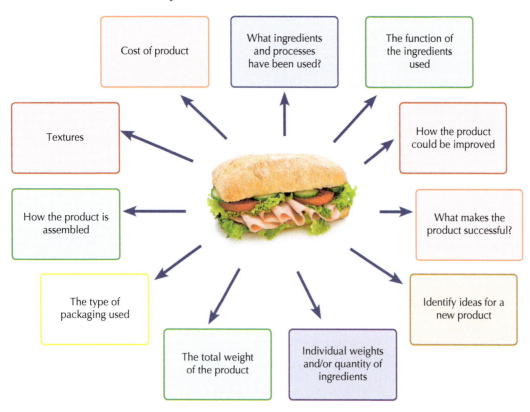

Cost of product

What ingredients and processes have been used?

The function of the ingredients used

Textures

How the product could be improved

How the product is assembled

What makes the product successful?

The type of packaging used

The total weight of the product

Individual weights and/or quantity of ingredients

Identify ideas for a new product

An example of a form for disassembling a sandwich

Product name	Cost	Total weight of product	Cost per 100g	Type of bread	Weight of bread	Weight of filling 1	Weight of filling 2	Weight of spread	Weight of sauces	Proportion of bread/ filling total weight
Sandwich 1										
Sandwich 2										

An example of a form for the packaging

Name of sandwich	Shape of packaging	Diagram of packaging with measurements	Number of sandwiches it holds	All statutory labelling on package	List of voluntary labelling
Sandwich 1					
Sandwich 2					

Let's Cook

Make up a batch of crunchy biscuits or scones, or use the breakfast cereal bar recipe below.

Breakfast cereal bar
Ingredients:

125g porridge oats

2 × 15ml melted syrup

50g brown sugar

50g margarine

50g dried fruit – sultanas or dried apricots (cut up) or cranberries

Method

1. Put on oven at Gas No 4 or 180ºC.

   Line a sandwich tin with foil.

   Collect ingredients.

2. Melt the margarine, syrup and brown sugar in a pan over a low heat until melted. Remove from the heat.

3. Mix in the porridge oats and fruit.

4. Place the mixture into the tin and smooth with the back of a tablespoon.

5. Place into the oven and bake for 20 minutes until golden brown. Leave in the tin for 5 minutes to firm up, then mark into 8 and leave to cool. Cut into wedges whilst still warm.

Adapt the recipe for your biscuits, scones or breakfast bar. Trial them by carrying out a simple peer evaluation of the flavour, colour and texture. Find out if the class would buy them if they were introduced in the supermarket.

Test your knowledge

1. Explain the following stages of product development:

   a. concept generation

   b. prototype production

   c. product testing

   d. product launch.

2. What is disassembly and who would use it?

3. Give four benefits to the manufacturer of carrying out disassembly.

4. State one reason why Trading Standards carry out disassembly.

Topic 2: Safe food production

Keeping the bugs at bay

Bust those bugs – the biggest enemies for food production are those food-poisoning bacteria and food-borne diseases caused by bacteria!

E. Coli 0157 is a food-borne disease.

Staphylococcus is a food-poisoning bacterium.

What is the difference between food-poisoning and food-borne diseases?

- In food poisoning the bacteria **multiply in the food before it is eaten**.

- With food-borne diseases, only a few bacteria need to be eaten and they then **multiply in the stomach and intestine**.

Food-poisoning bacteria	Food-borne bacteria
Salmonella	E. Coli 0157
Staphylococcus	Campylobacter enteritus
Bacillus Cereus	Listeria
Clostridium Perfringens	

Food poisoning is an unpleasant illness which usually happens within 1–36 hours of eating contaminated or poisonous food. Although the main symptoms, which can last for 1–7 days, are abdominal pain, diarrhoea, vomiting and nausea, there can be other symptoms such as fever and headache.

Food poisoning is caused by **bacteria** or their **spores** and **toxins**.

Bacterial food poisoning is the most common type of food poisoning and takes place when food is contaminated with **pathogenic** bacteria.

So what is a spore?

Spores are bacteria in a resting phase, they do not multiply and they do not die. It is only when they return to favourable conditions that they grow and multiply again.

Spores can be very resistant to heat – temperatures of 100°C or above are often needed to kill them. They are also resistant to high concentrations of chemicals.

So what is a toxin?

A toxin, produced by some bacteria, is a poison in the food which is difficult to destroy by normal cooking processes.

> ⚠ **Watch point**
>
> Bacillus Cereus is found in cooked rice and is one of the bacteria that forms spores. That is why advice about reheating and holding temperatures are important.

What conditions do bacteria like in order to grow?

Warmth

- 5°C–63°C is the **danger zone** – this is the best temperature range for bacterial growth.

- The best (optimum) temperature for growth is 37°C (body temperature).

To prevent growth

- Food should be thoroughly cooked to a core temperature of 75°C or above.

- Food should be reheated to 82°C.

- Refrigerators must be operate between 1° and 4°C.

- Freezers must operate at –18°C.

> ⚠ **Watch point**
>
> Remember that left-over food should only be reheated once.

Food

- Bacteria love high-risk foods – these are foods that can be eaten without further cooking and are perishable, i.e. require refrigerated storage, e.g. cooked meats/poultry, stews, gravies, stocks, dairy products, shellfish, cooked eggs and rice.

- Bacteria hate low-risk foods as they do not support bacterial growth, such as salt, sugar and acid. Jams, pickles and food preserved in syrup inhibit the growth of bacteria.

Moisture

Bacteria prefer a high water content to grow and many foods contain sufficient moisture for growth.

> ⚠ **Watch point**
>
> When a dried food has moisture added to it, e.g. custard powder, soup, rice, it must then be treated as a high-risk food and stored outwith the danger zone.

Time

Given the correct conditions, bacteria can divide in two every ten minutes – this process is called 'binary fission'. It is essential that high-risk food is kept in the danger zone for as short a time as possible.

Two other conditions that can affect bacterial growth are:

- **pH level:** the pH scale (0–14) measures the acidity or alkalinity of a substance. In general bacteria cannot grow in conditions that are too acidic, so the risk of food poisoning is reduced. A pH of 7 is neutral. Most bacteria will grow well at pH 7.

- **Oxygen:** aerobic bacteria require oxygen to grow. **Anaerobic** bacteria can grow without the presence of oxygen.

> 🔍 **Hint**
>
> Red kidney beans that are eaten raw or undercooked can occasionally cause food poisoning – the canning process destroys the toxin.

There are other causes of food poisoning such as:

Viruses

Viral food poisoning takes place when viruses are transmitted by water or food. Viruses require living tissue for growth and therefore do not multiply in food.

Chemicals

This takes place when food is contaminated by chemicals during growth, storage, preparation or cooking, e.g. pesticides or cleaning chemicals.

Vegetables

Vegetable poisoning may be caused by the natural toxins found in some vegetables which are poisonous to humans, e.g. deadly nightshade, death cap (which look like mushrooms) and toadstools.

Reasons for the increase in food poisoning

1. **Farming/food production**
   - Intensive methods of food production where large numbers of animals (e.g. battery hens) in a small space increase the risk of contamination and cross-contamination when infection occurs.
   - The increasing length of the food production chain increases the hazards as more people and processes are involved, along with transportation and storage.

2. **Eating outside the home**
   - More people are choosing ready-to-eat meals, take-aways or restaurant food. This increases risk as more people are involved in the handling of the foods.

3. **Shopping for food**
   - Chilled and frozen food that has been purchased but not transported home quickly in a cool bag/box can cause food poisoning as they are in the danger zone for too long.

4. **More income available**
   - More money available means more people are purchasing high-risk foods such as meat and dairy products.

5. **Preparing food in the home**
   - A greater number of meals for large celebrations are being prepared too far in advance and there is often insufficient cold storage.
   - Food being prepared and not cooled quickly enough increases the risk of food poisoning.

- Not reheating foods correctly to the core temperature of 82°C results in bacteria not being destroyed.
- The popularity of barbecued foods increases the risk as foods are often burnt on the outside and uncooked in the centre, leading to pathogenic bacteria surviving.
- Inadequate thawing of poultry increases the risk as the core temperature of the food is not always adequate to kill off pathogenic bacteria.
- Poor storage and preparation can lead to cross-contamination from raw to cooked foods.
- Foods left uncovered can lead to contamination by flies or animals.

> **⚠ Watch point**
>
> The general public are becoming more knowledgeable about food poisoning due to media coverage and as a result more cases are being reported.

How to get it right

Safe and hygienic food practices, whether at home or in food production, should be the same to prevent outbreaks of food poisoning.

The following **food preparation rules** should apply throughout.

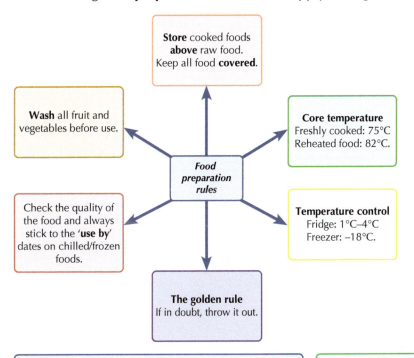

Food preparation rules

- **Store** cooked foods **above** raw food. Keep all food **covered**.
- **Wash** all fruit and vegetables before use.
- Check the quality of the food and always stick to the '**use by**' dates on chilled/frozen foods.
- **The golden rule** — If in doubt, throw it out.
- **Core temperature** — Freshly cooked: 75°C; Reheated food: 82°C.
- **Temperature control** — Fridge: 1°C–4°C; Freezer: –18°C.

Do

Wash hands after going to the toilet and before touching food – this will prevent food contamination.

Cover any cuts/boils with a blue waterproof plaster to prevent bacterial contamination of the food.

Tie hair back to prevent it falling on the food.

Wear clean protective clothing to protect the food from you!

Don't

Wear jewellery – it harbours bacteria.

Smoke – fingers touch the lips then the food, resulting in contamination.

Wear strong perfume – it taints the food.

Cough or sneeze over food – the mouth, nose and ears all contain bacteria.

Don't 'double dunk' spoons when tasting food as this can contaminate it.

What about the manufacturer/food producer?

A system called **Hazard Analysis Critical Control Point (HACCP)** has been developed to check food safety from the start to finish of the food chain.

The HACCP system has benefits for both the manufacturer and consumer.

Benefits for the manufacturer	Benefits for the consumer
Hazards are identified and controlled at each stage of food production and controls are put in place which help to prevent bacterial growth and food poisoning.	Food should be safer to eat so less risk of food poisoning.
Reduces the risk of having products recalled because of food safety issues. This would give the company bad publicity and sales would drop.	A consistent quality of product is provided, encouraging consumers to buy.

The seven stages involved in the HACCP system are as follows.

Stage 1: Conduct a hazard analysis

Potential hazards associated with **food** and control points are identified during this stage to control these hazards.

Possible hazards:

1. Contamination:
- biological, such as bacteria, moulds and viruses
- chemical, such as cleaning chemicals and pesticides
- physical, such as foreign bodies like glass, pests, metal.

2. Temperature control during storage: bacteria and mould will multiply if stored at a higher temperature than recommended.

3. Insufficient cooking: can lead to bacteria surviving.

Stage 2: Decide on the critical control points

The critical control points within a food manufacturing process are where controls can be applied to prevent, eliminate or reduce to an acceptable level any food safety hazards (for example temperature control with a high-risk food such as chicken).

A **control point** is when a hazard does not carry a food poisoning risk and therefore good hygiene practices at this stage should be sufficient to ensure food safety.

Stage 3: Establish a tolerance level

Controls must be implemented at this stage to eliminate the hazard or reduce it to a safe level. This stage establishes preventative measures with critical limits for each control point.

For example, for a cooked food the control might include setting the minimum cooking temperature and time required to ensure food poisoning bacteria are destroyed.

Stage 4: Establish a monitoring system

Procedures must be put in place to monitor the steps. This involves checking to make sure the controls are being implemented and are working effectively. Time and temperature are two very important factors and are relatively easy to monitor.

For example, refrigerator and freezer temperatures can be checked and the temperature noted at set times during the day.

Stage 5: Establish what action could be taken to correct the hazard if it occurs

When monitoring has revealed a problem or when a complaint is received, then action to correct the hazard must be taken (corrective action).

Some examples of corrective action include:
- Disposing of food if the minimum cooking temperature has not been met.
- Rejecting out of date stock.

Stage 6: Establish procedures to check that the HACCP system works effectively

An example of this could be testing a time and temperature recording device to verify that a cooking unit is working properly.

Stage 7: Record-keeping and review of procedures

This would include records of hazards, their control and the monitoring that has taken place.
It is a legal requirement to keep records of procedures followed. These records will be used as evidence to show 'due dilligence' in the event of a prosecution.

The areas during food production where HACCP is used:

- Purchase of ingredients
- Delivery of ingredients
- Storage of ingredients
- Preparation of ingredients
- Cooking of ingredients
- Chilled storage/cooling
- Packaging of the product
- Distribution of the product.

✔ Test your knowledge

1. Describe the difference between food-poisoning bacteria and food-borne diseases.
2. Identify and explain two conditions that bacteria need to multiply.
3. What should the core temperature of reheated food be?
4. Give two reasons for the increase in food poisoning.
5. State two personal hygiene rules you should follow during food preparation.
6. (a) What do the initials HACCP mean?
   (b) Explain why the HACCP system is used by the food industry.
7. What is the difference between a 'critical control point' and a 'control point'?
8. Describe the benefits to the consumer of the HACCP system.

Let's Cook

Make a chicken lasagne
Identify all the critical control points for this dish and come up with controls that should be observed.

Make a decorated fruit cheesecake and a spaghetti bolognese – observe the correct hygiene procedures throughout.

GO! End of chapter activities

Activity 1

Working in small groups: disassembly challenge – pizza

As a pizza manufacturer you are concerned to see that your own make of 'ham and pineapple' pizzas have had a recent drop in sales. You wish to discover the reasons for this.

You have decided to disassemble another two brands of pizzas and compare them against your own. Disassembly will help you to investigate the range and proportion of ingredients.

You must carefully weigh each ingredient as you disassemble.

You should disassemble three quarters of the pizza and cook the remaining quarter to allow for tasting.

Your comments should be as detailed as possible – they will help you decide how to improve your own pizza. A copy of this table can be downloaded from www.leckieandleckie.co.uk/n45health

	Your own pizza: Pizza A	Pizza B	Pizza C

Weight of ingredients
• Base
• Cheese
• Topping then
  • Ham
  • Fruit/vegetables
• Overall weight			

Comment on proportion of ingredients, e.g. ratio of topping to base, etc.			
Nutritional information per 100g • Fat • Salt • K cals			
Cooking time/storage			
Cost/value for money			
Comments on flavour			
Comments on texture			
Comments on appearance			
Rank each of the pizzas overall: 1–3, 1 being best			
Suggestions to improve your own pizza:			

Make the Link

See Chapter 6 for information about disassembly.

Activity 2

As a class

Watch the following video clips.

* www.food.gov.uk – select 'Business and Industry', then 'Food hygiene for businesses'. Click on HACCP, read the information, and then click on 'Training for food handlers'. Watch all or some of the 10 food safety coaching videos.
* Watch https://www.youtube.com/watch?v=LdGv-vQcacs

As a class, discuss each of the video clips and use the information to build a HACCP guide for the Home Economics room.

Activity 3

On your own

You have been asked to prepare chicken mayonnaise sandwiches for a buffet party in your own home.

Step 1

Explain how you would ensure good food safety whilst making and serving the sandwiches. Use the following headings to help you:

* Purchase of ingredients
* Storage of ingredients
* Preparation of ingredients
* Cooking of ingredients
* Storing and wrapping the sandwiches
* Serving.

Step 2

Draw up a simple HACCP system for the production of a chicken mayonnaise sandwich for a supermarket.

Activity 4

Watch some or all of the following clips from the BBC website by searching for the titles in a search engine:

* Food temperature
* Microorganisms and food
* pH and bacterial growth
* Seeing the bacteria carried on hands
* The importance of handwashing in food hygiene

As a class discuss each of the video clips. On your own, devise an A4 sheet of information on 'Hints to prevent the spread of bacteria onto food'.

Activity 5

On your own

A manufacturer has decided to produce a new chilled fruit dessert.
Complete the table below for each stage of the food product development process.

Stages of food product development	Describe each stage	Explain why each stage is important to the food manufacturer
Concept generation		
Concept screening		
Prototype production		
Product testing		
First production run		
Marketing plan		
Product launch		

Do this task well, as it could be kept for your portfolio of work. You must explain at least four of the food product development stages well.

? Exam-style questions

To help you prepare for the exam, remember to look at pages 191–202, Keeping on track: preparing for the National 5 course assessment.

Question 1

Identify and explain **two** conditions necessary for the growth of bacteria.　　　**4 marks**

Question 2

State **two** points to be considered when reheating food to prevent food poisoning.　**2 marks**

Question 3

A catering van has been inspected and the following have been found:

　　i.　Raw meat and vegetables being prepared using the same knife.
　　ii.　Hot food being placed in the refrigerator to cool down.

For **each** of these situations identify **one** potential food hygiene hazard and describe how it could be prevented.　　　　　　　　　　　　　　　　Total: **4 marks**

Question 4

Explain why a food manufacturer may carry out **each** of the following stages in product development:

    i.   Concept generation

    ii. Prototype production.   **2 marks**

Question 5

Give **two** reasons why a manufacturer would use disassembly.   **2 marks**

Now check your answers at the back of the book.

Rate your progress

How confident are you that you have achieved each of the following objectives?

Using the following key as a guide, give yourself a rating for each of the objectives below

Rating	Explanation
1	Confident with the standard of my work
2	Fairly confident with the standard of my work
3	The majority of my work was satisfactory
4	Require to do some further work
5	Require a lot of work

Objectives	Rating
Explain the stages of food product development	
Undertake investigations to generate ideas for food product(s) that meet specified needs	
Make prototype food products using safe and hygienic practices	
Conduct sensory evaluation of food products	
Explain how a food product meets specified needs	

Look at your ratings.

Write down two **next steps** to 'unlocking' your knowledge of food product development.

7 Developing food products to meet specified needs

After completing this chapter you should be able to:

- Carry out investigative techniques to generate ideas for food products that meet specified needs.
- Develop prototypes of food products.
- Conduct sensory evaluations of food products.
- Explain how the food product meets specified needs.

Make the Link

Throughout this chapter refer to Chapter 6.

Topic 1: Meeting the needs for new products

What is market research?

Market research is the activity of collecting and studying information about what people want, need and buy.

Why do manufacturers use it?

Manufacturers use it to find out:

1. What consumers want to buy or to gain consumers' opinions, e.g. whether there is a need for a particular product and if it will sell, such as snack-type foods, weight-reduction foods, etc.
2. If there is a gap in the market, i.e. is there a real need for the product?
3. What competition there is from other manufacturers.
4. The market trends, i.e. which foods are popular at a particular time.

When is market research carried out?

It can be carried out at any of the following times:

1. Before the development of a new product.
2. Throughout the development of a new product.
3. After the launch of a new product.

Hint

Market research is often carried out on existing products to evaluate their popularity, especially if there has been a drop in sales.

What are the benefits of market research?

- ✓ It helps food businesses plan how to promote and advertise a product.

- ✓ It helps the food industry find out about a new product idea before they spend too much money developing it.

- ✓ It allows manufacturers to establish if it will be profitable for them.

- ✓ It helps manufacturers keep track of market trends.

- ✓ Competition from other manufacturers will be identified.

Carrying out market research

Before starting it is important to:

1. Identify the gap in the market and the target group.
2. Brainstorm the information you want to find out.
3. Identify the most appropriate investigative techniques to use.

Step 1: Gap in the market identified

A manufacturer has identified a gap in the market for healthier wraps.

Step 2: Brainstorming information

Use this technique to help you come up with some points or needs you would have to consider when developing the healthy wrap.

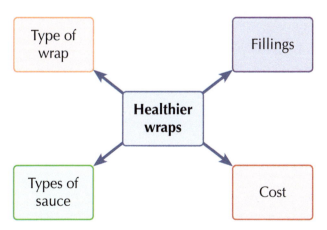

Step 3: Investigative techniques

Techniques that can be used to generate information within market research are:

A: Questionnaire

How to develop a questionnaire

Think about what you would like to find out, then decide on the **type** of questions you will need to ask and the **target group** you will be using (i.e. the group of people you are developing the new product for).

🔍 Hint

When carrying out a questionnaire, manufacturers must ask a large number of people to complete it.

Type of wrap

1. *What kind of wrap do you prefer?* ☐

   White ☐
   Wholemeal ☐
   Sun-dried tomato ☐
   50/50 ☐
   Olive ☐

Fillings

2. *What kind of fillings do you prefer? (Tick two)*

   Chicken ☐   Grated carrot ☐
   Ham ☐   Lettuce ☐
   Beef ☐   Onion ☐
   Bacon ☐   Cucumber ☐
   Roasted vegetables ☐   Cheese ☐
   Tomato ☐   Prawn ☐
   Sweetcorn   Tuna ☐

Types of sauce

3. *Which of the following sauces do you prefer? (Tick one)*

   Mayonnaise ☐
   Curried mayonnaise ☐
   Marie Rose sauce ☐
   Salad cream ☐
   Guacamole ☐
   Sour cream ☐
   Pickle ☐

Cost

4. *How much would you pay for a wrap?*

   No more than £1.50 ☐
   No more than £2 ☐
   No more than £2.50 ☐
   No more than £3 ☐
   No more than £3.50 ☐

These are all 'closed' questions. They are the best type of questions to use as they give a range of possible answers, making it easier to collate, present and analyse the results.

Collate the numbers beside each question and then present in a table format.

B: Research: survey, literary/internet research

The first thing to do is identify the **source(s) of information** you will be using. This could involve:

- Going to a variety of supermarkets or food outlets.
- Visiting food outlets to find out the existing range of 'healthy option' wraps.
- Using the internet.
- Literary search – research using books/recipes/magazines/newspaper articles.

Collate and present a summary of all the information gathered under appropriate headings such as 'type of wrap used'.

C: Interviews

The suitability of the person to be interviewed should be carefully considered to ensure you get accurate and useful information.

This type of research can take the form of more 'open-ended' questions to allow more information to be collected from the person being interviewed.

Example

Person being interviewed – supermarket manager.

Question – Which types of wraps are the most popular?

Collate and present the results of all the questions and answers used.

✔ Test your knowledge

1. State when manufacturers could carry out market research.
2. Give a reason why market research is sometimes used on existing products.
3. Explain each of the following investigative techniques:
   - questionnaire
   - survey
   - interview.

Topic 2: Testing the senses

Sensory testing

The overall acceptability of a product is extremely important to food manufacturers.

Sensory testing/analysis is a very important part of food product development as it helps manufacturers to find out about the following:

- The acceptability to the consumer of a food when developing a new product
- How it compares against a competitor's product
- The shelf-life through testing of the product at various recommended storage points
- Quality control to ensure consistent standards across batches
- Monitoring of prototypes
- Whether changes to an existing product, e.g. reduction in salt, affects the eating quality
- What makes a product popular
- How to reduce the cost without affecting the flavour.

There are certain procedures to be followed when carrying out sensory testing of a product to ensure the results gained are consistent – these are called '**controlled conditions**'.

Procedures to follow for sensory testing

Procedures	Reason
✓ Always check that everyone taking part is able to taste the product. ✓ Do not allow people who are unwell (colds, upset stomachs) to taste.	✓ Some people may have allergies or dietary conditions preventing them from carrying out the tasting. ✓ They may spread infection and they will not be able to taste the food properly.
✓ Ensure good hygiene. Everyone to use clean spoons after every testing. Disposable cutlery should be used and thrown away after each tasting.	✓ This prevents the spread of infection between people tasting the food.
✓ Serve all food samples in the same way (i.e. same plate, portion size and temperature).	✓ This ensures the food is fairly compared.
✓ Label the foods with either random letters or numbers.	✓ To prevent people from being able to identify the food samples.
✓ Only allow tasters to test up to a maximum of six samples at a time.	✓ The taste buds become less effective the more you taste.
✓ Have water available to sip between tastings.	✓ This will clear the palate and make tastings more effective.
✓ Complete the tasting charts after each food is tasted.	✓ The taster will forget his/her opinion if all tasting is done at once.
✓ Use separate booths with the same level of lighting.	✓ This ensures the tasters do not influence each other and the level of light does not influence the look of the food.

Types of sensory test

Different types of tests are used to obtain different kinds of information. There is, however, a set of standard tests which can be used by the industry.

Group 1: Preference tests

These are used to supply information about peoples' likes and dislikes for a food product, e.g. 'smoothness'.

Tests included in this group are:

Tasters taking part in a sensory test.

Ranking test

In this test the tasters are asked to rank in order of preference a range of similar food products, e.g. tomato soup made by different manufacturers or processed by different methods. The results are recorded in a table such as the example below.

Products	Order of preference	Any comments
A		
B		
C		
D		
E		

Rating test

This test allows people to show how much they like or dislike several aspects of a variety of products. In this test, foods may be given a score of 1 to 5 as follows:

1. Like a lot
2. Like a little
3. Neither like nor dislike
4. Dislike a little
5. Dislike a lot

Products are sometimes scored on a 9-point scale.

People sampling the products may complete a chart similar to the one below.

Rating test	Product A	Product B	Product C
1. Like a lot			
2. Like a little			
3. Neither like or dislike			
4. Dislike a little			
5. Dislike a lot			

Pictures are often used for children to make it easier for them to understand. They are asked to tick the box under the face which best describes how they feel about the product.

Rating score	1	2	3	4	5
Product A					
Product B					
Product C					

Group 2 – Discrimination tests

These tests are used to find out:

- The difference between similar products.
- The difference if the proportions of ingredients are changed, e.g. if salt levels are reduced.

Tests included in this group are:

Paired comparison test

In this test the tasters are asked to compare two samples for a specific characteristic, e.g. flavour or seasoning of the dish.

Triangle test

In this test tasters are given three samples, two of which are the same, and they are asked to identify the odd one out.

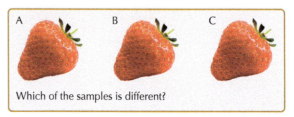

Which of the samples is different?

Taste threshold test

This test finds the sensitivity of the taster to a particular taste. For example, the taster might be asked how much water can be added to squash before the flavour becomes too weak.

Profiling test or star profile – these are ways of recording or presenting results

Manufacturers use this method to compare their own products with other competitors' brands to find out why other brands are more popular with consumers and have larger sales figures. This allows them to find out how they need to improve their own product.

Star diagrams enable detailed descriptions to be gathered of a variety of aspects of a food product. A star shape is drawn, with each line divided into, usually, five sections. Sometimes seven or nine sections are used in each line.

A descriptor is identified at the end of each line. The descriptor used will depend on the aspects of the product being tested.

The tasters would have carried out a rating test based on each descriptor and then the results are collated as shown in the sample below.

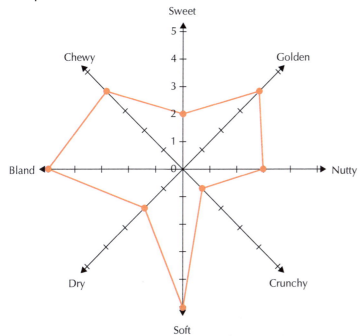

Any changes to the product can be made. For example, sensory testing may have revealed that the food is not sweet enough, so the ingredients may have to be changed.

《 Let's cook

- Prepare a decorated gateau then carry out a rating test as a **class** to find out which gateau is the best for appearance.
- Market research has shown that cheesecake is a popular dessert. As a class develop and make a cheesecake recipe which takes account of at least **two** aspects of current dietary advice.

✓ Test your knowledge

1. Give four reasons for carrying out sensory testing.
2. Identify two procedures to follow during sensory testing and explain why they are used.
3. Describe the difference between a ranking and a rating test.
4. Explain how to carry out a triangle test.
5. State one reason why a manufacturer would use a profiling test.

GO! End of chapter activities

Activity 1

Working on your own, in pairs or groups

> **Brief**
> The school snack canteen area has identified the need for a new take-away soup which would be suitable for the staff and pupils.

Step 1

Brainstorm the brief to identify the important points that need to be considered. Using this information identify **two needs** from the brief.

Step 2

Use at least **two** different techniques (e.g. questionnaire, interview or survey) to gather information about these identified needs, e.g.

- A **questionnaire** should have at least five appropriate closed questions and be issued to a minimum of 10 pupils/staff.
- An **interview** should have at least five relevant questions that you could ask the school cook.
- A **survey** of the local supermarket or a food outlet could be carried out to find out the existing range of take-away soups.

Step 3
- Collate and present the information you have gained from the two investigations.

Step 4
- Come up with a recipe for the new soup or soups and give reasons for your choice based on the results of the questionnaires.

Step 5
- Make the soup or soups (if you are working in pairs or groups).

Step 6
- Develop a sensory evaluation sheet to record the results of a rating test.

Step 7
- Carry out a sensory evaluation of your soup(s) using a minimum of five people.
- Record the results and write a conclusion based on the results of the sensory evaluation.

Step 8
- Explain how the soup meets or does not meet the two needs you identified in Step 1 of this activity.
- You should make at least **two** relevant comments.

Do this task well if you are working on your own, as it could be kept for your portfolio work.

Activity 2

Work through each sensory test for a given product (e.g. cereal bars/breakfast cereals).

Test 1: Ranking test

Taste all the samples and place them in order of preference with regard to **flavour**.
1 = the one you like the best, 5 = the one you like least. The tables below can be downloaded from www.leckieandleckie.co.uk/n45health

Product	Order	Comments
A		
B		
C		
D		
E		

Test 2: Rating test

Taste the samples and circle the number which best describes the product with regard to overall liking of **texture**. 1 = best, 5 = worst.

Rating	Product A	Product B	Product C	Comments
1. Like a lot	1	1	1	
2. Like a little	2	2	2	
3. Neither like nor dislike	3	3	3	
4. Dislike a little	4	4	4	
5. Dislike a lot	5	5	5	

Test 3: Paired comparison test

Taste the two samples for **palatabilty** and try to tell the difference between them.

Product	Comments on palatability
A	
B	

Test 4: Triangle test

Identify the odd one out by ticking the box.

Product	Tick	Comments
A		
B		
C		

Which one is the odd one out?

To sum up

Discuss the results with the rest of the class.

Activity 3

Working in pairs

Find out what is meant by 'changing market trends' in food product development.
Identify a range of food products that have been continually adapted and improved to meet the changing market trends (e.g. bread).

Activity 4

As a class

- Make up a star profile for a cheese and tomato flan to include the following descriptors:
  - Taste
  - Appearance
  - Crispiness of pastry
  - Colour
  - Texture of filling.
- Make the flan.
- Ask someone at home to give a rating for each of the above descriptors.
- As a class, collate the results and complete a star profile for the cheese and tomato flan.

❓Exam-style questions

To help you prepare for the exam, remember to look at pages 191–202, Keeping on track: preparing for the National 5 course assessment.

Question 1

A chef is developing a new healthy fruit smoothie for his restaurant's children's menu.

The results of sensory testing are shown below. Choose the **most suitable** healthy fruit smoothie for the chef to make.

Fruit smoothie A

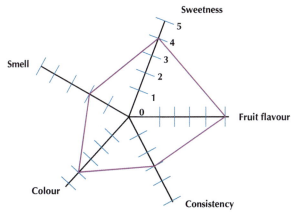

Fruit smoothie B

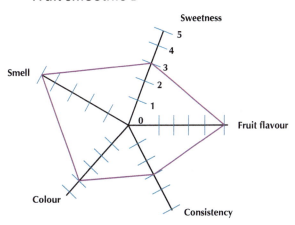

Fruit smoothie C

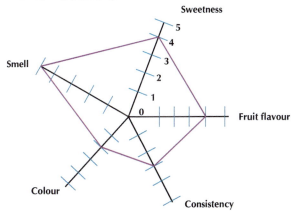

Key: 1 = poor, 5 = excellent.

i. Choose the **most suitable** healthy fruit smoothie for the chef to make.

ii. Give **three** reasons for your choice.

4 marks

Question 2

Identify **two** sensory tests the manufacturer could carry out on a new product.

Explain the information the manufacturer would gain from **each** of these.   **4 marks**

Question 3

Describe **two** ways market research could benefit a manufacturer when developing
a new product.   **2 marks**

Now check your answers at the back of the book.

Rate your progress

How confident are you that you have achieved each of the following objectives?

Using the following key as a guide, give yourself a rating for each of the objectives below

Rating	Explanation
1	Confident with the standard of my work
2	Fairly confident with the standard of my work
3	The majority of my work was satisfactory
4	Require to do some further work
5	Require a lot of work

Objectives	Rating
Carry out investigative techniques to generate ideas for food products that meet specified needs	
Develop prototypes of food products	
Conduct sensory evaluations of food products	
Explain how the food product meets the specified needs	

Look at your ratings.

Write down two **next steps** to 'unlocking' your knowledge of food product development.

This unit will develop your knowledge and understanding of factors which may affect consumers' food choices. You will look at contemporary food issues, technological developments and food labelling and how they may influence food choices. Consumer organisations that protect the interests of the consumer are also be included in this unit.

Practical activities will allow you to produce food products which take account of some of the factors which affect consumers' food choices.

By the end of this unit you should be able to:

OUTCOME 1: EXPLAIN CONSUMER FOOD CHOICES.

This means you have to:

- Explain factors which may affect consumers' choice of food.

- Explain contemporary food issues which may affect consumers' choice of food.

- Describe technological developments which may affect consumers' choice of food.

- Describe how organisations protect the interests of consumers.

- Explain how information on food labels help consumers make informed choices.

OUTCOME 2: MAKE A FOOD PRODUCT WHICH ADDRESSES ISSUES AFFECTING CONSUMER FOOD CHOICES.

This means you have to:

- Select an issue which may affect consumer food choices.

- Explain a food product which addresses this issue.

- Make a food product and explain how it addresses this issue.

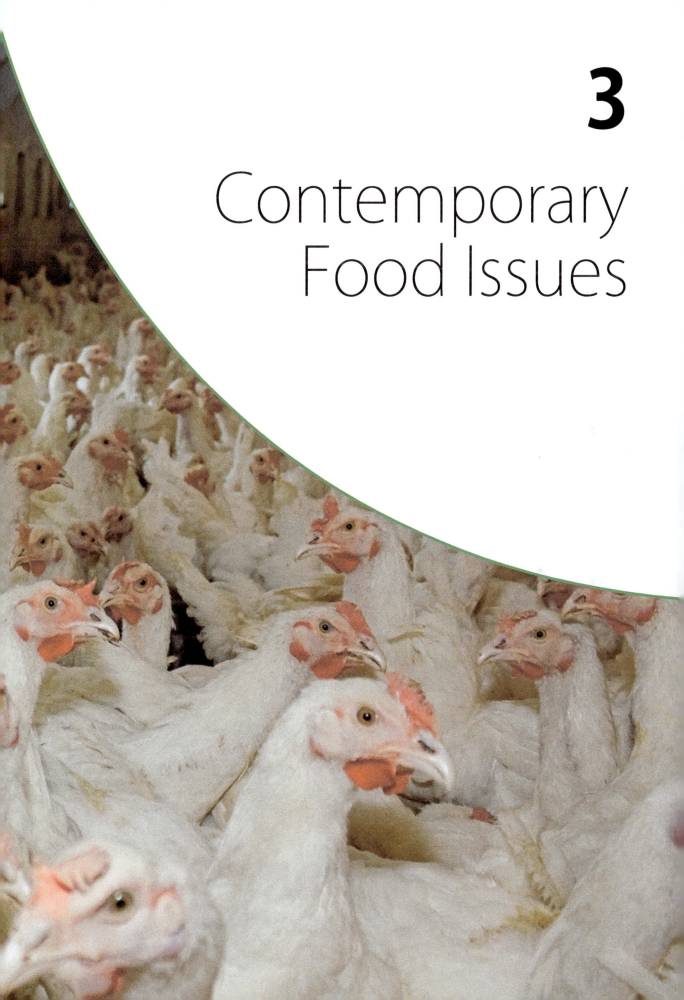

3

Contemporary Food Issues

8 Factors affecting consumer food choice

After completing this chapter you should be able to:

- Explain each of the following factors and how they may affect a consumer's choice of food:
  - budget
  - online shopping
  - lifestyle
  - working hours or shift patterns
  - nutritional knowledge
  - special dietary needs
  - allergies
  - foreign travel and knowledge of world cuisine
  - likes and dislikes
  - peer pressure
  - advertising and the media.
- Make food products which address factors affecting consumer food choices.
- Explain how food products take account of these factors.

Make the Link

Throughout this chapter refer to Chapters 9 and 10.

Topic 1: Main factors which may influence food choice

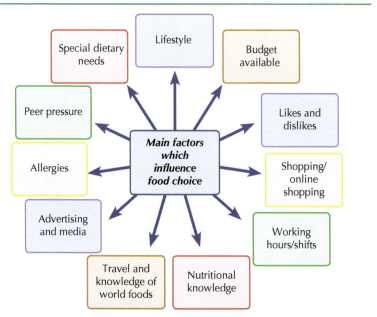

Let's look at how each of these factors could affect consumers' food choices.

Budget available

- More high fat or high sugar foods may be chosen if the budget is limited, as these are popular so will not go to waste.

- The amount of fruit and vegetables bought may be reduced as they are expensive and if they are not eaten then they are wasted.

- Consumers who have a restricted income may choose shop's own budget range of food, which is cheaper than named brands.

- Healthier alternatives to everyday foods may be too expensive for families on a limited income (e.g. wholemeal bread, spreads low in saturates).

- Special offers, e.g. 'buy two get one free', money-off vouchers in supermarkets can save money but care must be taken, as these offers often promote unhealthy foods.

- Foods are often reduced in supermarkets as they near their 'use by' date and can often be frozen at home to be used later.

Online/internet shopping

- Longer opening hours and 24-hour shopping in supermarkets means that consumers will always have access to a range of foods.

- Many consumers order their food shopping online, which saves them time when they are busy. It is also useful for disabled or housebound people.

- Online shopping allows the consumer time to compare prices from the comfort of their own home.

- The food is delivered straight to the door and delivery times can be selected which are convenient to the shopper.

- This method saves the hassle of standing in a queue and having to load and unload the shopping at the checkout.

- Delivery charges are added, which does increase the cost.

- Because consumers don't choose their own products, foods sometimes can have short 'use by dates' and fruit and vegetables may not be of the best quality.

- Consumers may worry about the security of paying for goods over the internet.

Lifestyle

- Working parents and single parent households may have less time for meal preparation when they come home. More ready meals may be used as a result.

- A lack of practical food preparation skills may lead to more take-away or convenience foods being bought.

- There are an increasing range of take-away and fast food outlets which produce a large selection of ready-to-eat foods for consumers.

- Snacking and grazing are common throughout the day. Consumers want food that is easily consumed on the move, e.g. snack foods, breakfast bars, ready-made sandwiches.

- Families may choose to eat out more often as many food outlets have special offers such as money-off vouchers, 'kids eat free' deals or loyalty cards.

- An increase in television cookery programmes has promoted more home cooking.

Hint

Lifestyle may also be influenced by families' budgets.

Working hours or shift patterns

- More mothers work, so may choose foods children can prepare themselves.

- Shift work can result in families eating at different times of the day and as a result they rely more on convenience foods.

- Workers can quickly microwave frozen or cook-chill meals when they come home or they can take them to work.

- Due to busy lifestyles or shift patterns many families don't sit down together for a meal.

Nutritional knowledge

- Consumers with little nutritional knowledge may choose less healthy options, which may increase their risk of developing dietary diseases.

- The traffic light system and guideline daily amounts (GDAs) may help some consumers to make healthier choices.

- Some nutritional labelling may be difficult to understand and lead to unhealthy choices.

- Manufacturers produce many 'healthy options' which can be confusing as they may be low in fat but high in sugar.

Special dietary needs

- Special dietary needs can be linked to:
    - diet-related diseases
    - food intolerances or allergies
    - the dietary needs of individuals at different stages of their lives.

- Some religions have dietary rules which may influence food choice as certain foods may be forbidden or can only be eaten on particular occasions, e.g.

    - **Hindu:** The cow is considered a sacred animal so Hindus will not eat beef; pigs are considered unclean, so pork is not eaten either.

    - **Muslim:** Muslims are forbidden from eating pork, and animals have to be ritually slaughtered by a process known as Halal.

    - **Jewish:** Jewish people only eat Kosher meats (meat slaughtered in a special way), and are forbidden from eating shellfish and, like Hindus and Muslims, pork.

- Cultural influences have led to an increase in the range of foodstuffs from other countries available in the supermarket.

☀ Make the Link

Look at Chapters 3 and 4 for more information on dietary needs.

Travel and knowledge of world cuisine

- The increase in travel both at home and abroad may encourage people to be more adventurous in their eating habits.

- An increased range of ethnic foods and restaurants gives consumers more variety.

Likes and dislikes

- If food looks, smells and tastes good then consumers are more likely to choose it.

- As many products are available in single portions, individual likes and dislikes within families can also be catered for – this is useful if someone in the family is a vegetarian.

Peer pressure

- Children often choose the same foods as their peers to fit in with their friends' likes and dislikes.

- Consumers may choose different foods from their peers just to show individuality.

Advertising and the media

- Television has the biggest influence on food choices.

- Manufacturers will target their products at certain groups. This can be done in a number of ways, e.g.

  - free toys or games with children's food products

  - celebrities, cartoon characters or jingles to promote food products

  - humorous, catchy and easily remembered adverts

  - sponsorship of events and television programmes, e.g. sport/soaps.

- Legislation is now in place to prevent the advertising of foods high in fat, sugar and salt during the peak hours of children's viewing, to discourage them from eating too many of them.

Let's Cook

Scottish culture
Prepare a dish using traditional Scottish ingredients, e.g. haggis lasagne, or choose a different culture.

Test your knowledge

1. Choose one television food advert you have seen recently. How did the advertiser try to make the food appeal to consumers?
2. Explain two ways in which advertising may affect consumers' choice of food.
3. State two advantages of online shopping.
4. Explain how religion can affect a consumer's food choices.

GO! End of chapter activities

Activity 1: Fresh versus convenience

Work in pairs

Compare a number of products made using fresh ingredients with similar convenience ones. Some examples could be:

- Tomato soup/carrot and coriander soup
- Chilli con carne/lasagne
- Trifle/fruit cheesecake
- Muffins/scones.

You would need to draw up a comparison chart which could look like the one below, depending on your product. You could use a rating test of 1–5 for taste, appearance and texture where 1 = best and 5 = worst. A copy of this chart can be downloaded from www.leckieandleckie.co.uk/n45health

Product: _____	Fresh	Convenience	Comments
Time to prepare			
Time to cook			
Cost			
Taste			
Appearance			
Texture			
Cost			
Energy value			
Shelf-life			

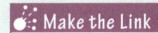

:: Make the Link

Look at Chapter 7 for ideas for sensory testing.

Activity 2

Watch some of the adverts produced by Marks & Spencer. Go to http://www.marksandspencer.com Select 'M&S TV' at the bottom of the web page. Select 'Food' and then choose an advert. **Working in pairs**, discuss some of the techniques that have been used to promote the products.

Working in small groups

Produce a one-minute television advert for a new food product. The advert should:
- be aimed at a particular target group
- persuade your target group to buy your product.

You will then present the advert to the class.

Activity 3: Revision guide

Working in groups

Research the factors on pages 133–136 which may affect consumers' food choices and come up with a Powerpoint presentation that the whole class could use for revision.

Step 1

In groups, brainstorm how each factor could affect food choice.

Step 2

The teacher will give your group the factors to work on so that they are all covered by the class.

In your group decide who will work on each of the factors, either on your own or in pairs.

Use some of the textbooks available in the room or use the internet.

Step 3

Create a Powerpoint presentation showing how the factors affect consumers' choice of foods. The presentation should be:

- easy to follow
- colourful
- informative.

Step 4

Each group should present the factors they have been given. The rest of the class should listen carefully to see if any additional points need to be added.

Step 5

The class's work could be put onto the school website so that you can all use it for revision.

Activity 4

Working on your own

You are now going to carry out practical activities linked to some of the factors affecting food choice. You should also use the knowledge you gained from Unit 1 (Food for Health), as each of your dishes must be healthy.

Lifestyle

- You are rushing home to get ready for your weekly swimming class and you don't have a lot of time. Prepare a quick vegetarian snack for yourself. Explain why your food product is suitable for this situation.
- You think your friend eats too much take-away Indian food. You are going to prepare your own Indian take-away to show her that it can be quickly prepared as a 'make at home' dish. Explain how your food product could change her lifestyle.

Shift work

- Your brother works shifts. Prepare a pasta dish for him to reheat in the microwave at work.
- Explain how your food product is suitable for someone who works shifts.

Budget

- Anne is a student living on a limited budget. Prepare an economical cold dish using left-over cooked chicken that would fit in with her budget.
- Explain why your food product is suitable for someone on a limited budget.

Travel and knowledge of world cuisine

- You have just returned from a holiday in Italy. Prepare a dish using a traditional Italian ingredient. Explain how your food product shows the use of foods from another country.
- Your school lunch canteen is having a Mexican day. Prepare a fajita or taco that could be served from the snack area of the canteen. Explain how your food product shows the use of foods from another country.

Likes and dislikes

- Your younger sister does not like vegetables. Prepare a dish that 'hides' the vegetables so that she would eat it. Explain how your food product would encourage her to eat more vegetables.
- The children at your local nursery are taking the 'Eat 5 a day veg pledge'. Make some vegetable snacks with a dip that they could try. Explain how your food product would encourage nursery children to eat more vegetables.

? Exam-style questions

To help you prepare for the exam, remember to look at pages 191–202, Keeping on track: preparing for the National 5 course assessment.

Question 1

Explain how **each** of the following factors could influence a consumer's choice of food.

   a) Religion

   b) Lifestyle   **2 marks**

Question 2

A young single male who has a full-time job and often works overtime at weekends wants to do his weekly food shopping online.

Evaluate the suitability of the following method of online shopping for him.

Online shopping

Food items arranged in alphabetical order
Weekly special offers available
System remembers previous order
Substitute items sent automatically
£5 delivery charge
Morning, afternoon or evening delivery slots
Delivery available Monday to Saturday

                                                       4 marks

Question 3

Explain **one** way each of the following might affect a consumer's choice of food.

   a) Peer pressure

   b) Shift patterns   **2 marks**

Now check your answers at the back of the book.

Rate your progress

How confident are you that you have achieved each of the following objectives?

Using the following key as a guide, give yourself a rating for each of the objectives below

Rating	Explanation
1	Confident with the standard of my work
2	Fairly confident with the standard of my work
3	The majority of my work was satisfactory
4	Require to do some further work
5	Require a lot of work

Objectives	Rating
Explain each of the following factors and how they may affect a consumer's choice of food: • budget • online shopping • lifestyle • working hours or shift patterns • nutritional knowledge • special dietary needs • allergies • foreign travel and knowledge of world cuisine • likes and dislikes • peer pressure • advertising and the media	
Make food products which address factors affecting consumer food choices	
Explain how food products take account of these factors	

Look at your ratings.

Write down two **next steps** to 'unlocking' your knowledge of contemporary food issues.

9 Contemporary food issues affecting consumer food choice

After completing this chapter you should be able to:

- Explain each of the following contemporary food issues and how they may affect a consumer's choice of food:
  - factory farming; farmers' markets; allotments
  - genetic modification (GM); organic produce
  - food miles; seasonality
  - packaging; recycling; pollution
  - Fairtrade.
- Make food products which address issues affecting consumer food choices.
  - Select an issue which may affect consumer food choices.
  - Explain a food product which addresses this issue.
  - Make a food product and explain how it addresses this issue.
- Explain how the food products take account of these factors.

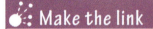 **Make the link**

Throughout this chapter refer to Chapter 8.

Hint

Meat, poultry, eggs and milk can all be produced by factory farming.

Topic 1: Factory farming; farmers' markets; allotments

What is factory farming?

- Factory farming is the term used to describe a farm which operates like a factory rather than like a farm where animals are reared naturally.

- The aim of factory farming is to produce the largest quantity as cheaply as possible.

- As many animals as possible are crammed together in a small space where feeding, watering and clearing of waste are all done automatically.

How can consumers' food choices be affected?

Why consumers may choose factory farmed produce	Why consumers may not choose factory farmed produce
• Foods produced this way can be cheaper. • Consumers are unaware of the conditions the animals are reared in.	They are concerned about: • animal welfare due to the conditions they are kept in • possible animal diseases spreading, which can be passed on to humans • the use of antibiotics, pesticides and growth hormones may find their way into the human food chain.

What are farmers' markets?

These are usually open air markets where farmers sell fresh, locally grown seasonal produce. Some consumers prefer to buy foods from these local markets where animal care has been considered, e.g. free range chicken and eggs.

There are also more continental-themed food markets being introduced, allowing consumers to try foods from other countries.

How can consumers' food choices be affected?

Why consumers may choose food from farmers' markets	Why consumers may not choose food from farmers' markets
• There is a range of fresh, local and healthy produce. • There are less food miles as the produce is local. • The amount of packaging used is reduced. • There are more organic and less intensively produced foods available.	• Some foods may not be available, it depends on the time of year. • Foods may be more expensive.

What are allotments?

In the UK allotments are small pieces of measured land rented to people, usually for the purpose of growing fruit and vegetables.

Grow your own in the UK is the up and coming initiative!

🔍 Hint

Allotments are good for the environment as food grown on them have fewer food miles and require fewer pesticides and fertilisers.

How can consumers' food choices be affected?

Why consumers may choose to grow their own food in allotments	Why consumers may not choose to grow their own food in allotments
• Fruit, vegetables and herbs are fresher – they can be picked and used as and when required. • More nutritious – no loss of vitamin C due to storage. • Cheaper to grow your own than buy from a supermarket. • Can be a great hobby – healthy exercise, fresh air, reduces stress.	• Lack of knowledge, skills, time or interest in growing their own food.

Let's Cook

The local farmer sends his vegetables – carrots, potatoes, leeks, broccoli, onions, cabbage – to a farmers' market to be sold. Using some of these ingredients as a base, make a soup for tasting at his stall.

Test your knowledge

1. Explain two advantages to the consumer of buying food from the local farmers' market.

2. Explain two benefits to the consumer of the grow your own initiative.

3. Describe two ways in which factory farming could influence food choice.

Hint

There are many arguments for and against using GM products. Keep up to date by reading the newspapers, watching TV or through the internet.

Topic 2: Genetic modification (GM); organic produce

Genetic modification (GM)

What is genetic modification?

- Characteristics of plants or animals, such as colour, size, shape and growth, are carried in the genes. These are passed on to the next generation.

- GM foods have usually been artificially changed by scientists in a laboratory.

- Genetic modification is done by transferring genes between plants and animals. For example, genes can be transferred from one plant to another, from a plant to an animal or from an animal to a plant, to produce certain changes and improvements, e.g. making a plant more pest-resistant.

Although no GM crops are grown in the UK at present, European Union (EU) law requires any approved GM products to be clearly labelled, including ingredients that have come from other countries, e.g. soybean, maize, tomatoes.

How could consumers' food choices be affected?

For GM foods	Against GM foods

• **Nutritional value** may be improved:
  • vitamin C and E in fruit and vegetables can be changed to contain higher levels
  • leaner meat that is lower in saturated fat can be produced
  • protein can be increased in the rice and maize grown in poorer countries of the world.
• Can help to **preserve** food:
  • longer shelf-life for fruit and vegetables, which reduces waste
  • controlling crop diseases, so reducing loss.
• Gives consumers more **choice**:
  • improved quality, flavour, appearance and texture, e.g. tomatoes, potatoes
  • vegetarian cheese can be produced by GM, therefore increasing food choice.
	• No one knows the long-term effects on the human body.
	• Foods are not always clearly labelled as containing GM ingredients. A very low level of GM ingredients have found their way into some processed foods.
	• Strict vegetarians would object to eating foods which contain animal genes.
	• Muslims, Sikhs and Hindus have ethical and religious objections to consuming foods which contain genes from animals.
	• There are concerns about the effect on the environment – genetically modified plants and animals could affect wildlife and animal welfare.

Organic produce

What is organic produce?

Organic food is food which has been produced to standards which keep the production more 'natural'. The term '**organically grown**', when applied to meat, dairy products, fruit and vegetables, should mean that:

- **Artificial chemical fertilisers** are not used – animal and vegetable waste materials are used as fertilisers.

- **Pesticides are severly restricted** – organic farmers develop nutrient-rich soil to grow healthy crops and encourage wildlife to help control pests and diseases.

- **Animal welfare** is important and farm animals have a **free-range life**.

Processed foods claiming they are organic should contain at least 95% organic ingredients.

The **Soil Association** is the main body in the UK to certify food and producers as organic and check whether the required standard is met.

By identifying the Soil Association logo on food packaging, consumers are able to select foods that have been grown without artificial fertilisers, which may be good for those with allergies. It can help those consumers select foods that have been made without man-made chemicals, which may be harmful to health.

How could consumers' food choices be affected?

Why consumers **may choose** organic foods	Why consumers **may not** choose organic foods
• They believe they taste better. • Some consumers believe them to be more nutritious than non-organic foods. • They believe they are free from chemicals or pesticide residues and are therefore better for health, with fewer side effects or allergies. • They believe that less harm is caused to the environment and animal welfare is improved. • To make it easier, some smaller producers now deliver boxes of organic fruit and vegetables to your door.	• Organic foods tend to be expensive and are therefore not available to low-income groups. • They believe no nutritional benefit is gained so the extra money spent is a waste. • The appearance may be less attractive, especially vegetables, so many consumers will not buy them. • Fruit and vegetables may not keep for so long due to the lack of pesticides or preservatives, so could result in more being wasted.

Let's Cook

You are going to taste and compare organic with non-organic foods.

When you finish tasting answer the following questions:

1. Overall, which of the foods – organic or non-organic – had the better taste, texture and colour?

2. Look at the cost of each food and decide which products offer the best value for money.

Test your knowledge

1. Give a simple explanation of genetic modification of food.

2. Discuss two reasons why consumers may not want to include GM food in their diet.

3. Explain three advantages of organic foods.

4. Explain two reasons why consumers may not want to buy organic foods.

Topic 3: Food miles; seasonality

Food miles

What are food miles?

Food miles are the total number of miles your food has travelled from where it is grown to your plate.

How are consumers' food choices affected?

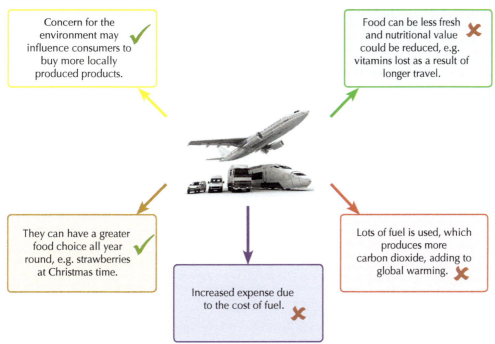

Concern for the environment may influence consumers to buy more locally produced products. ✓

Food can be less fresh and nutritional value could be reduced, e.g. vitamins lost as a result of longer travel. ✗

They can have a greater food choice all year round, e.g. strawberries at Christmas time. ✓

Increased expense due to the cost of fuel. ✗

Lots of fuel is used, which produces more carbon dioxide, adding to global warming. ✗

Seasonality

How are consumers' food choices affected?

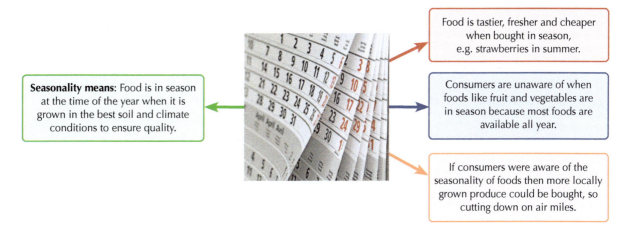

Food is tastier, fresher and cheaper when bought in season, e.g. strawberries in summer.

Consumers are unaware of when foods like fruit and vegetables are in season because most foods are available all year.

If consumers were aware of the seasonality of foods then more locally grown produce could be bought, so cutting down on air miles.

Seasonality means: Food is in season at the time of the year when it is grown in the best soil and climate conditions to ensure quality.

Let's Cook

Go to the British Nutrition website www.nutrition.org.uk and search 'Why eat seasonally?' Choose a season – spring, summer, autumn or winter – and see which foods are at their best at that time.

Find a recipe that includes at least one food which is in season, e.g.

- spring – cauliflower, cabbage
- summer – rhubarb, plums
- autumn – courgettes, carrots
- winter – leeks, potatoes.

Make the Link

Refer to Chapter 12: food labelling.

⚠ Watch point

Disadvantages of packaging foods

- Can add to the cost of the product.
- Over-packaged foods can take up more storage space in the cupboard.
- The type of packaging used could be an environmental concern.

Topic 4: Packaging; recycling; pollution

Packaging

Packaging has a number of functions.

I: *Information*

- Useful information so consumers can make an informed choice.
- How to store and use food safely.
- Enables the food to be easily recognised.

M: *Marketing*

- Packaged in convenient sizes and/or weights.
- Attractive and colourful to encourage consumers to buy.

P: *Protection*

- Helps keep the food undamaged while being carried home.
- More hygienic – protects the food from bacteria, and people cannot touch the food.
- Improves food safety through the use of tamper-proof packaging.
- Easier to transport home and store.

Types of packaging used

Material	Recyclable?	Advantages	Disadvantages
Glass	Yes	• Strong • prevents loss or gain of moisture and oxygen, which can affect food quality • can be transparent so contents are seen • made in a variety of shapes and sizes • does not react with food • re-usable in the home.	• Easily broken • heavy to carry home.
Paper or cardboard	Yes	• Can be reasonably strong depending on the quality • can be printed on easily • light to carry home.	• Does not protect food from moisture • crushes or tears easily.
Metal – aluminium and steel tins; tin foil	Yes	• Strong and rigid • good barrier to moisture and gases • can be printed on easily • tin foil is strong and can be moulded round awkward shapes of food.	• Tin cans for acidic foods must be coated on the inside to prevent a reaction • can be heavy to carry home.
Plastic – rigid	Some	• Lightweight but reasonably strong • waterproof • made in a variety of shapes and sizes • most do not react with food • can be used in a microwave	• Has to be sorted into different types before recycling. Some types are not recyclable.
Flexible, e.g. clingfilm		• cling film can be moulded round awkward shapes.	• Clingfilm is not very strong and is difficult to use. Cannot be re-used or recycled.

Some packaging is made from more than one material, e.g. Tetra packs are made from several layers of fine plastic, a layer of aluminium and cardboard. It is a rigid packaging and is used for cartons of drinks, custard etc.

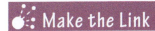

Make the Link

Go to chapter 10 for information on another type of packaging called Modified Atmosphere Packaging (MAP).

Developments are always being made to introduce new types of packaging to keep up with technological developments, e.g. freezer to ovenproof containers.

Consumers who are concerned about the environment will consider the type of packaging when buying products.

Recycling and pollution

Some packaging is not environmentally friendly.

Manufacturers are being encouraged to help protect the environment by cutting down on the amount of packaging used and by using recyclable packaging materials. Biodegradable packaging is preferable as it will easily break down in the soil or the atmosphere.

Some types of recyclable packaging are:

- Netting/flow wrap/film wrap/moulded cartons – these are more environmentally friendly due to biodegradable materials.

- Recycled paper.

- Glass and some plastic containers – these help save energy due to fewer CO_2 emissions and reduced waste at landfill sites, and can be reused around the home.

- Refills for some products, saving on packaging.

- Loose products using less packaging, e.g. fruit, bakery goods.

Check the plastic packaging

When shopping, check for recycling symbols on the packaging and try to buy these products.

Some packaging made from certain plastics cannot be recycled so has to be sent to landfill, which can contaminate the land, or be incinerated, which can pollute the air with poisonous gases produced when burned.

Recycling symbols

Recycling symbols on packaging are useful to the consumer as they allow them to choose food packaging which is less harmful to the environment.

Some common recycling symbols:

Glass		Shows the product can be put in a bottle bank to be recycled. Glass can be used again to make 'new' glass, which is cheaper to produce.
Aluminium		Recyclable aluminium is more environmentally friendly and will help reduce costs for future consumers. This is cheaper than starting from new and helps to conserve energy.
Tidy man		Used to encourage people to recycle and dispose of in a bin to protect the environment. It is used most often on snack foods such as crisps and cans of drink.
Plastics		Various types of plastic are available. The type of plastic is identified below the triangle.
Paper or card packaging		This symbol (called the mobius loop) means that a product or part of it can be recycled. In the centre of the loop sometimes the percentage of recycled material contained in the product is shown.
On-pack recycling label scheme		The on-pack recycling label scheme aims to deliver a simpler, UK-wide, consistent, recycling message on both retailer private label and brand-owner packaging to help consumers recycle more material, more often.

Let's Cook

Recycling also applies to left-over food.
Use left-over cooked potatoes to make fish cakes or potato scones.
Make a curry sauce to use up left-over vegetables and meat.

✔ Test your knowledge

1. You have left-over soup, cooked chicken and apple pie. Identify a different type of packaging for each of them. Explain your reasons for choosing the packaging.
2. Give two reasons why packaging is important.
3. Name three types of materials that can be recycled.
4. Descibe two ways shoppers could reduce the amount of packaging they buy.
5. What is the tidy man symbol used for?
6. What does 'biodegradable' mean?

Topic 5: Fairtrade

Fairtrade

What is Fairtrade?

The purpose of the Fairtrade system is to improve the wages and working conditions of workers in developing countries who produce the goods.

By buying products that carry the Fairtrade Mark, shoppers know that disadvantaged producers and workers in developing countries are getting a better deal: receiving a fair price for their products as well as an additional amount to invest in their businesses and communities.

How are consumers' food choices affected?

For Fairtrade	Against Fairtrade
• The quality of foods can be better because Fair Traders consider the environment.	• As Fairtrade products may be transported from far-off countries, some consumers are concerned about food miles.
• The Fairtrade Mark is clearly marked on food products to help consumers with their choice.	• Some shops stock a limited range of Fairtrade products so the consumer has less choice.
• There is a range of food products for consumers to choose from – bananas, coffee, chocolate, tea.	• Some Fairtrade products tend to be expensive and some consumers may not be able to afford them.
• Fairtrade products can be obtained from a variety of sources, e.g. Fairtrade stores, supermarkets, catalogues and websites.	

🔍 Hint

The Fairtrade system includes environmental standards. This requires producers to work to protect the natural environment by using environmentally-friendly practices.

☑ Test your knowledge

1. State the main purpose of the Fairtrade system.

2. Describe two ways consumers' food choices could be affected by Fairtrade products.

3. Explain two disadvantages of Fairtrade products to the consumer.

☕ Let's Cook

Prepare a baked item which could be used at a Fairtrade coffee morning.

Use the recipes in the department and substitute Fairtrade ingredients where appropriate, e.g. coffee buns, banana cakes, chocolate traybake.

GO! End of chapter activities

Activitity 1

Working in pairs: factory farming

Watch the two short cartoons at http://www.themeatrix.com/ called The Meatrix. These will give you information about factory farming.

After watching each of the cartoons, make notes about the **concerns** of factory farming in the chart below.

Question or prompt	What I thought	What my partner thought	What we will share
What are the concerns of factory farming?			

Think

On your own, think about the concerns of factory farming.

Pair

Exchange answers with a partner.

Share

Share your answers with other pairs or the whole class.

Conclusion

Is factory farming for you?

Activity 2

As a class

Watch the Food Miles and Wastage UK Video, which you can find by using a search engine.

On your own

Answer the following questions.

1. *How many miles in total have each of the following foods travelled?*

Food	Country	Miles
Apples	USA	
Trimmed green beans	Kenya	
Red seedless grapes	Chile	
Lamb	New Zealand	
Mango	Peru	
Potatoes	Israel	
King prawns	Indonesia	
Tomatoes	Canary Islands	

2. *If you used all these foods to make a meal, how far has your meal travelled?*

Activity 3

Watch all or some of the following short video clips, which you can find by typing the names into a search engine like Google.

- Recycle more and give things another life – Scottish Government video
- Audition for metal recycling – Natural Scotland video
- Audition for paper and cardboard recycling – Natural Scotland video
- Audition for glass recycling – Natural Scotland video
- Audition for plastic recycling – Natural Scotland video

Working in groups

The school eco group has been asked to do a presentation to encourage recycling in school. Your group should work on one aspect of recycling. To contribute to the whole presentation you could produce a Powerpoint, short play or song to get the recycling message over. You may also find useful information at www.greenerscotland.org.

Activity 4

Working in pairs

Technological developments in packaging have allowed manufacturers to present their products in more convenient ways for consumers to use.

Identify **two** food products which use **each** of the following methods.

- Moulded plastic trays
- Shrink wrap
- Resealable packs
- Sqeezable containers
- Pull-tab-to-open containers
- Easy-pour cartons

Activity 5

On your own

Select one contemporary food issue which may affect consumers' choice of food, e.g. the number of **food miles** a food travels may concern some consumers. Produce a food product which takes these concerns into account. Explain how your product has addressed the food issue you chose.

Activity 6

On your own

Recently you have become more 'food aware', i.e. more aware of where and how the food you are eating is produced.

a. Choose three of the following food issues:
- factory farming
- organic produce
- Fairtrade
- seasonal foods.

b. Produce a poster that explains the three food issues and how they may influence your food choice.

Do this task well if you are working on your own, as it could be kept for your portfolio of work.

? Exam-style questions

To help you prepare for the exam, remember to look at pages 191–202, Keeping on track: preparing for the National 5 course assessment.

Question 1

Explain **three** advantages to the consumer of packaging foods. **3 marks**

Describe **one** disadvantage to the consumer of packaging foods. **1 mark**

Question 2

Explain **two** ways environmental issues might affect a consumer's choice of food. **2 marks**

Question 3

A couple who both work full-time wish to buy a weekly organic fruit and vegetable box. They enjoy cooking and entertain regularly.

Evaluate the suitability of the following box for the couple.

Organic fruit and vegetable box
- Random selection of fruit and vegetables which will vary weekly.
- Free delivery.
- Delivery Monday to Saturday 9.00am–6.00pm.
- All produce grown within a 20-mile radius.
- Can order online.
- Recycling symbol on cardboard box.

4 marks

Now check your answers at the back of the book.

Rate your progress

How confident are you that you have achieved each of the following objectives?

Using the following key as a guide, give yourself a rating for each of the objectives below

Rating	Explanation
1	Confident with the standard of my work
2	Fairly confident with the standard of my work
3	The majority of my work was satisfactory
4	Require to do some further work
5	Require a lot of work

Objectives	Rating
Explain each of the following contemporary food issues and how they may affect a consumer's choice of food:	
• factory farming; farmers' markets; allotments	
• genetic modification (GM); organic produce	
• food miles; seasonality	
• packaging; recycling ; pollution	
• Fairtrade	
Make food products which take account of factors which affect consumer food choices	
• Select an issue which may affect consumer food choices	
• Explain a food product which addresses this issue	
• Make a food product and explain how it addresses this issue	
• Explain how the food products take account of these factors	

Look at your ratings.

Write down two **next steps** to 'unlocking' your knowledge of contemporary food issues.

10 Technological developments affecting consumer food choice

After completing this chapter you should be able to:

- Explain each of the following technological developments and how they may affect a consumer's choice of food:
  - food additives
  - chilling and cook-chill products
  - UHT products; Modified Atmosphere Packaging (MAP)
  - functional foods
  - developments to meet dietary needs.
- Make food products which address technological developments affecting consumer food choices.
- Explain how food products take account of technological developments.

> **⚬ Make the link**
>
> Throughout this chapter refer to Chapters 3 and 4.

Topic 1: Food additives

It's all in the 'number'

Additives are natural or synthetic substances which are added in small quantities to foods during manufacture. They are added to foods for a particular purpose.

Many packaged foods contain additives – these are listed in the ingredient list on the food label.

All additives used in the UK have been strictly tested before being added to food.

Additives have an **E** number which shows that they have been accepted as safe by the countries of the European Union.

Many manufacturers may promote their products as additive-free, which may be preferred by consumers for a variety of reasons.

How do additives affect consumers' food choices?

Advantages of additives

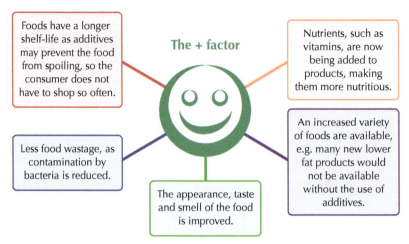

Foods have a longer shelf-life as additives may prevent the food from spoiling, so the consumer does not have to shop so often.

The + factor

Nutrients, such as vitamins, are now being added to products, making them more nutritious.

Less food wastage, as contamination by bacteria is reduced.

The appearance, taste and smell of the food is improved.

An increased variety of foods are available, e.g. many new lower fat products would not be available without the use of additives.

But additives are not popular with some consumers for the following reasons:

- Some types of additives cause hyperactivity in children.
- There are health concerns about long term use of some additives.

The main types of additives

Preservatives
- These help to keep food safer for longer by protecting it from micro-organisms like bacteria.
- The shelf-life of foods is longer so prevents wastage of food for consumers and retailers.
- They allow manufacturers to transport food in bulk, which is cheaper and keeps cost down for consumers.
- They are used in: baked goods, bacon and ham, soft drinks and fruit juices.

Antioxidants
- These give foods a longer shelf-life by protecting against deterioration caused by exposure to air.
- They prevent fatty foods from becoming rancid, which gives the food an 'off' flavour and makes them unpleasant to taste.
- They prevent cut fruit, vegetables and fruit juices going brown and so increase their shelf-life and appearance.
- They are used in dried soups, cheese spreads and sausages.

Colourings
- These replace the colour in foods, which may be lost during processing, so improving appearance and making foods more acceptable to consumers.
- Improve the natural colour of certain foods to make them more attractive.
- Some colourings may cause allergic reactions or irritate sufferers of asthma or eczema.
- Hyperactivity and behaviour problems in children can also be caused by some colourings.

Emulsifiers and stabilisers
- These additives prevent ingredients separating and give a smooth, creamy product, e.g. low-fat products can be produced such as low-fat spreads and salad dressings, as these allow fats and oils to mix with water, so reducing the fat content.
- They allow manufacturers to produce products which can remain stable, i.e. not separate out during transport and on the shop shelf.
- Emulsifiers help improve the shelf-life of baked goods.

Flavourings
- These are added to foods in small amounts to improve the taste and smell, e.g. vanilla could be added to ice cream.
- Used to produce artificial flavours in foods where 'real' flavours may add to the cost (e.g in yoghurt, strawberry flavouring is cheaper than adding fresh strawberries).
- These can make flavours in some foods stronger, e.g. monosodium glutamate (MSG) will intensify the flavour of other ingredients. Some people may be allergic to MSG.

Sweeteners
- Saccharin and aspartame are used in products instead of sugar and only a little is needed, as they are many times sweeter than sugar.
- They are added to products to reduce the sugar and calorie content, so would be helpful to people who are trying to lose weight.
- They are used in low-calorie drinks and reduced-sugar foods.
- The long-term effects on health are unknown.

✔ Test your knowledge

1. Give a definition of an additive.

2. Explain two reasons why additives are used in food products.

3. Explain one advantage and one disadvantage to the consumer of each of the following additives: colourings; sweeteners; flavourings.

4. Baby food manufacturers claim that their foods are additive free. Why would parents choose these products?

🔍 Hint

Where a flavouring is used rather than a fruit in yoghurt, manufacturers are not allowed to use a picture of the fruit on the label.

Let's Cook

Prepare a dessert which uses raspberries, blackberries or blueberries as a natural colouring, e.g. fruit mousse, yoghurt fool.

Make a birthday cake for a hyperactive child that avoids using artificial colourings.

> ### 🔍 Hint
> Remember that the temperature of the refrigerator at home should be no more than 4°C – use a fridge thermometer to check.

Topic 2: Chilling and cook-chill products

What are chilled and cook-chilled products?

Chilled food is prepared food that is stored at refrigeration temperatures, which are at or below 8°C to prevent bacteria multiplying, e.g. cold meats, salad, sandwiches.

Cook/chill foods include ready meals and desserts. They are cooked in the factory and then chilled in blast chillers to remove the heat quickly and prevent the growth of bacteria.

How are consumers' food choices affected?
Cook-chill meals and chilled products may be popular with consumers because

The + factor

Foods are usually easy to use, prepare, cook/reheat in a microwave and so can save time in a busy life.

They can work out cheaper than buying individual ingredients to make the same dish. Good for students and people living on low incomes.

There is a wide selection from which to choose, e.g. ethnic, vegetarian, so giving variety in the diet.

Chilling does not affect food quality, colour, flavour, texture or nutritional value, making the product more acceptable to the consumer.

There are a variety of price ranges, e.g. supermarket basic or value through to 'finest' ranges, to suit different budgets.

Many cook-chill meals can be frozen at home so save on shopping time and are good for emergencies.

People with little or no cooking skills or who have difficulty preparing and cooking meals, e.g. the elderly, can use them as they only require reheating.

> ### 🔍 Hint
> Many supermarkets are using cook-chill meals as part of their meal-deal promotions.

Cook-chill meals and chilled products may not be popular with some consumers because

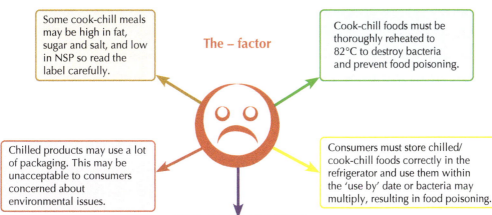

Some cook-chill meals may be high in fat, sugar and salt, and low in NSP so read the label carefully.

The – factor

Cook-chill foods must be thoroughly reheated to 82°C to destroy bacteria and prevent food poisoning.

Chilled products may use a lot of packaging. This may be unacceptable to consumers concerned about environmental issues.

Consumers must store chilled/cook-chill foods correctly in the refrigerator and use them within the 'use by' date or bacteria may multiply, resulting in food poisoning.

If using cook-chill meals for a number of people then it can work out more expensive than cooking from scratch.

⚠ Watch point

Many cook-chill meals are now using recyclable packaging, which appeals to the consumer.

✔ Test your knowledge

1. Give a definition of cook/chill products.
2. Why must 'use by' dates be observed by consumers?
3. To what temperature must a cook-chill ready meal be heated and why?
4. Explain four benefits of cook-chill products to the consumer.

Let's Cook

Prepare a pasta dish which could be sold as an individual salad pot in the chilled cabinet of a supermarket.

Prepare a dish that could easily be reheated in the microwave and would appeal to children.

Topic 3: UHT products: Modified Atmosphere Packaging (MAP)

What are UHT products?

- UHT is a sterilising process in which foods are rapidly heated to approximately 140°C and held at that temperature for a few seconds to kill any bacteria present.

- The products are then quickly cooled and packed.

- Examples of UHT products are long-life milk and fruit juice.

How could consumers' food choices be affected?

- UHT products have a longer shelf-life which allows them to be stored for longer.

- They are convenient to store as they do not need to be refrigerated unless opened. Once opened they have to be treated in the same way as fresh foods.

- They are handy to have in the store cupboard in case of emergencies.

- UHT milk can taste different from fresh, so some consumers may not like the flavour.

Modified Atmosphere Packaging (MAP)

One of the most popular technological developments in packaging with consumers is Modified Atmosphere Packaging, or MAP.

What is MAP?

- Manufacturers can change the type of gas inside packaging to improve shelf-life. MAP replaces most of the oxygen in packs with carbon dioxide and nitrogen.

- The growth of bacteria and micro-organisms is slowed down because the oxygen has been removed.

- MAP is used in ready-prepared salads, cook-chill meals, fresh pasta, meat and poultry, bacon, snack products like crisps, and baked products like rolls and cakes.

How could consumers' food choices be affected?

Water resistant and does not allow the gas to escape. This improves the storage of food and prevents it drying out. ✓

Correct storage instructions have to be followed after opening to prevent the foods spoiling and being wasted. ✗

The use of natural gases appeals more to customers. ✓

Shelf life of food is improved as the oxygen content is reduced. ✓

The amount of packaging used may be an environmental concern for consumers. ✗

Product can be seen through the packaging before buying. ✓

Better quality food has to be used. ✓

Vacuum packing

Another type of packaging that has the air removed is vacuum packaging. The plastic package is then sealed. This type of packaging is used for bacon and fish.

✔ Test your knowledge

1. Describe two advantages of UHT products to the consumer.
2. Name two food products which are packed using MAP.
3. Explain how MAP helps to preserve foods.
4. Give two ways MAP may affect consumers' food choices.

Let's Cook

Using a bread product, e.g. tortilla wraps, baguette, bagels, pitta, naan bread, make a savoury snack which would be suitable to be packed using MAP.

Prepare a pasta dish that includes fresh pasta and one other food packed using MAP.

Topic 4: Functional foods

What are functional foods?

Functional foods contain ingredients that have health-promoting properties. The term 'functional foods' can cover a range of products such as: spreading fats, yoghurts, drinks.

Functional foods cannot make health improvement claims unless they have medical evidence to back their claim.

Spreading fats

Spreading fats such as Benecol currently form one of the biggest functional food sectors in the UK. Substances called plant sterol esters are included in these spreads to help lower blood cholesterol levels, particularly 'bad' cholesterol, and reduce the risk of heart disease.

Some spreads provide omega-3 fatty acids from fish oils which, if present in sufficient quantities, will contribute to the prevention of heart disease.

Vegetarians may be unaware of the use of fish oils in spreading fats.

Make the link

Refer to Chapter 1 for more information on 'bad' cholesterol.

Yoghurts

Yoghurts and yoghurt drinks which contain probiotic or 'friendly' bacteria may help to maintain the natural balance of the digestive system and act as an aid to digestion.

Cereals and grains

Breakfast cereals, cereal bars and bread are fortified with vitamins and minerals, which will improve health.

Drinks

Drinks may be fortified with the antioxidant vitamins A, C and E and some contain caffeine, which claims to improve physical performance.

How are consumers' food choices affected?
Functional food products may be popular with consumers because

Functional foods may improve health and reduce the risks of certain diseases when taken as part of a balanced diet and healthy lifestyle.

The + factor

Allows consumers to take greater control of their health through choosing functional foods for specific health benefits.

Some foods, e.g. breakfast cereals and bread, are a reasonably inexpensive source of additional minerals and vitamins in the diet.

If there is a family history of heart disease, using a functional spreading fat (which contains plant sterols) could help control cholesterol within the family.

🔍 Hint
It is possible to get the same benefits more cheaply and naturally by eating a balanced diet.

But there are some disadvantages to functional foods

- Functional foods would have to be eaten in a fairly large quantity and for a long time to result in any improvement to health.

- Functional foods can be quite expensive, which may prevent low-income consumers from buying them.

🍲 Let's Cook

dippy dunk challenge
- Develop a breakfast cereal bar/cookie that uses the functional foods cereals and spreading fats.
- Develop a dip using probiotic yoghurts.
- Come up with a name for your product to promote the benefits from the functional ingredients.

☑ Test your knowledge

1. **(a)** What are functional foods?
   (b) Explain two advantages of functional foods to the consumer.
   (c) Explain one disadvantage of functional foods to the consumer.

2. **(a)** Identify two groups of people who could benefit from functional foods.
   (b) Explain why these foods may be useful for each group.

Topic 5: Developments to meet dietary needs

Sweeteners (often referred to as sugar substitutes)

The main types of sweeteners are:

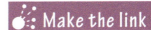

> **Make the link**
>
> Refer to the text on additives on pages 159–161.

- **Intense sweeteners**, e.g. saccharin and aspartame, which can be used in soft drinks, canned foods and as sweeteners for tea and coffee.

- **Bulk sweeteners**, e.g. sorbitol, which can be used in jams for diabetics.

😊 Consumers may choose sugar substitutes because	😦 Consumers may not choose sugar substitutes because
😊 They can reduce the sugar and calorie content of the diet, so helping weight reduction.	😦 Sometimes they can leave an unpleasant aftertaste in the mouth.
😊 Can be used in the 'healthy option' market to reduce the energy value of these products.	😦 Some people have concerns about sweeteners as their long-term effects on health are unknown.
😊 They are used in confectionery, bakery goods and many other foods, increasing the range of healthy options available, and this gives the consumer a wider choice of products.	😦 They are less suitable for food preparation – recipes have to be adapted to give good results.
😊 Bulk sweeteners are used in sugar-free confectionery and can help reduce the risk of tooth decay and obesity.	
😊 Some sugar substitutes are used in products suitable for diabetics, e.g. jams/jellies.	

Alternative protein foods: mycoproteins, soya proteins

A number of protein foods have been developed as meat substitutes and are particularly useful in vegetarian diets.

Mycoproteins (Quorn™)

What is Quorn™?

Quorn™ is a registered trademark for mycoprotein. It is made from a tiny fungus (like a mushroom), which is then fermented, mixed with egg white and flavours and then processed.

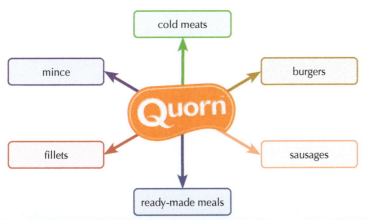

How are consumers' food choices affected?

Mycoprotein products may be popular with consumers because:

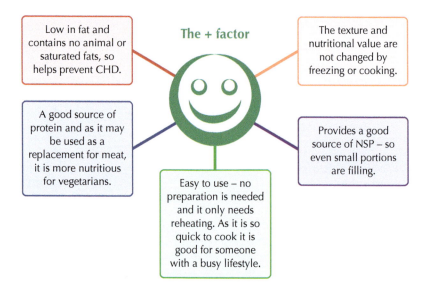

Low in fat and contains no animal or saturated fats, so helps prevent CHD.

The + factor

The texture and nutritional value are not changed by freezing or cooking.

A good source of protein and as it may be used as a replacement for meat, it is more nutritious for vegetarians.

Provides a good source of NSP – so even small portions are filling.

Easy to use – no preparation is needed and it only needs reheating. As it is so quick to cook it is good for someone with a busy lifestyle.

But there are some disadvantages to mycoproteins

- It does not contain vitamin B12, so vegetarians who use this product would have to gain their vitamin B12 intake elsewhere.

- Some products may contain egg white, which may make them unsuitable for vegans – read the label.

Soya proteins
Soya proteins are made from soya beans. Soya protein products include soya milk, margarines and in 1970 a meat-like product called textured vegetable protein (TVP) was produced.

Textured vegetable protein (TVP)
What is it?

- Textured vegetable protein or TVP is made from soya bean flour that has had its oil removed. The soya flour is mixed to a dough with water, put through a process where it is dried and then made into different shapes that look like mince or chunks. It needs to be mixed with water before use. Manufacturers have also made TVP burgers, sausages and ready-to-eat meals.

How are consumers' food choices affected?

TVP products may be popular with consumers because

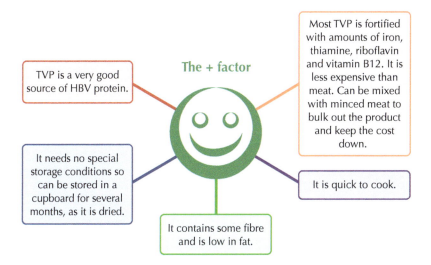

TVP is a very good source of HBV protein.

The + factor

Most TVP is fortified with amounts of iron, thiamine, riboflavin and vitamin B12. It is less expensive than meat. Can be mixed with minced meat to bulk out the product and keep the cost down.

It needs no special storage conditions so can be stored in a cupboard for several months, as it is dried.

It is quick to cook.

It contains some fibre and is low in fat.

But there are some disadvantages of TVP

- Can be lacking in flavour unless a strong flavour, e.g. chilli or curry powder, is added.

- Has a different texture to meat, which some people may not like.

Tofu

Tofu (right) is a food made by coagulating or setting soya milk and then pressing the resulting curds into soft white blocks. There are many different varieties of tofu, including fresh tofu, such as silken or block, and tofu that has been processed in some way. Tofu can be used in savoury and sweet dishes. It is often seasoned or marinated to suit the dish, e.g. in stir fries.

✔ Test your knowledge

1. Evaluate the nutritional value of mycoproteins.
2. Explain two disadvantages of mycoproteins.
3. Explain two advantages of using TVP.
4. Explain the difference between bulk and intense sweeteners.

Let's Cook

- Prepare a baked item using a sugar substitute. The following website will give you some ideas: http://www.splenda. co.uk/recipes. Some suggestions are: scotch pancakes, cupcakes, scones or muffins.

- Make a dish using tofu, e.g. a stir fry.

End of chapter activities

Activity 1

Working on your own

On your own, produce a leaflet on functional foods to hand out to staff in the school. Use the internet and any suitable books or leaflets to help you carry out research.

You should include:

- the range of functional foods available
- adverts/pictures of functional foods to show what is available
- the advantages of functional foods
- the disadvantages of functional foods.

You could use IT to develop the leaflet, which should be clear and well presented.

How well did you do?

After you have finished your information leaflet, swap your leaflet with another pupil in the class. They will give feedback on the quality of your leaflet using the chart below.
Read the statement that describes the leaflet and **circle** then **total** the score.

The leaflet should include	Description	Score	Description	Score	Description	Score
The range of functional foods available	A wide range	3	A good range	2	More could have been included	1
Adverts/pictures of functional foods	Very well illustrated	3	Good selection	2	Could have had more illustrations	1
Advantages of functional foods	Advantages are detailed and accurate	3	Most advantages are detailed and accurate	2	Could have been more detailed and accurate	1
Disadvantages of functional foods	Disadvantages are described in accurate detail	3	Disadvantages are mostly described in accurate detail	2	Could have been more detailed and accurate	1
Be clear and well presented	Clear and well presented	3	Mostly clear and well presented	2	Could be improved	1

Give advice on how the leaflet could be improved and then hand your evaluation and the leaflet back.

Activity 2

Working in small groups

Develop a healthy single portion cook-chill dish which can be reheated in a microwave. You will then have to give a 60-second 'pitch' to promote your product.

Step 1

Brainstorm some ideas for your product, e.g. think of ingredients that would be suitable for reheating in a microwave.

Come up with a possible idea for your product.

Step 2

Find a recipe that you could adapt easily to make your cook-chill product.

Give your product a name.

Step 3

Make your product and photograph it.

Step 4

Working in your group you should create a Powerpoint presentation or a design/storyboard to promote your cook-chill product.

Step 5

Deliver your presentation to the other groups.

Activity 3

Working in pairs

Carry out a survey of the additives used in packaged foods. Look at a range of packaged foods.

- Find any additive free foods.
- Identify products that contain additives.
- Try to work out the type of additives and the reasons why they have been used in the product.

Activity 4

Class activity

Go to http://www.bbc.co.uk/schools/gcsebitesize/design/foodtech/packaginglabelling_act.shtml and watch the video clip.

On your own

Answer the following questions:

- Which five different types of materials are used for packaging?
- How does MAP work?
- Which food products use MAP?
- How are food products affected?
- State two functions of packaging.

Activity 5

On your own or in pairs, make the following recipe for white chocolate and lime tofu cheesecake.

Ingredients

75g crushed ginger nut biscuits, 30g unsalted butter, 1 lime, 15g caster sugar, 75g silken tofu, 30ml whipped cream (soft peak), 35g white chocolate (suitable for cooking), 80g natural yogurt.

Method

1. Melt the butter and mix in the crushed biscuit crumbs.

2. Press the mixture into lined ramekins (or a 15cm flan ring) and place into the fridge to chill.

3. Wash, then grate the rind of the lime and squeeze out the juice. Reserve until required.

4. Beat the tofu and sugar together.

5. Melt the chocolate and mix with the tofu mixture.

6. Add the lime rind and 15ml of the juice to the tofu mixture and beat to incorporate.

7. Fold in the natural yogurt and half of the whipped cream and add to the tofu mixture. Reserve the remaining cream for piping.

8. Spoon the tofu mixture over the biscuit base and chill until it is firm.

9. Remove from ramekins if lined, and place on a cold plate.

10. Pipe the remaining cream, decorate appropriately and serve.

Which dietary needs/conditions are met by the ingredients in this recipe?

Taste the cheesecake with regard to taste, texture and appearance. Suggest any changes to improve the result. A copy of this chart can be downloaded from www.leckieandleckie.co.uk/n45health

---

On your own

Complete the following chart on how consumers' food choices may be affected by technological developments.

Technological development	How consumer food choice may be affected
Functional foods	
Food additives	
Cook-chill products	
Modified Atmosphere Packaging (MAP)	

Do this task well as it could be kept for your portfolio of work. You must have explained at least two technological developments well.

❓Exam-style questions

To help you prepare for the exam, remember to look at pages 191–202, Keeping on track: preparing for the National 5 course assessment.

Question 1

Explain how **each** of the following issues could influence a consumer's choice of food:

a) Food additives

b) Functional foods. **2 marks**

Question 2

Describe **two** benefits to the consumer of using mycoprotein. **2 marks**

Question 3

Technological developments have resulted in an increase in products using Modified Atmosphere Packaging (MAP).

Explain **two** advantages of MAP to the consumer. **2 marks**

Question 4

Explain **two** benefits to the consumer of buying cook-chill foods. **2 marks**

Now check your answers at the back of the book.

Rate your progress

How confident are you that you have achieved each of the following objectives?

Using the following key as a guide, give yourself a rating for each of the objectives.

Rating	Explanation
1	Confident with the standard of my work
2	Fairly confident with the standard of my work
3	The majority of my work was satisfactory
4	Require to do some further work
5	Require a lot of work

Objectives	Rating
Explain each of the following technological developments and how they may affect consumers' choice of food:	
• food additives	
• chilling and cook-chill products	
• UHT products; Modified Atmosphere Packaging (MAP)	
• functional foods	
• developments to meet dietary needs	
Make food products which address technological developments affecting consumer food choices	
Explain how food products take account of technological developments	

Look at your ratings.

Write down two **next steps** to 'unlocking' your knowledge of contemporary food issues.

11 Organisations that protect the interests of consumers

After completing this chapter you should be able to:

- Describe how the following organisations protect the interests of consumers:
  - Advertising Standards Authority
  - Trading Standards
  - *Which?*
  - Citizens Advice Bureau
  - Environmental Health Department
  - Food Standards Agency.

What are my rights as a consumer?

Products and services must be:

- **of satisfactory quality** – last for the length of time you would expect and be free of any defects
- **fit for purpose** – fit for the use described
- **as described** – match the description on packaging or the description of the service offered.

Topic 1: Advertising Standards Authority, Trading Standards, *Which?*

ASA – Advertising Standards Authority
www.asa.org.uk/

The ASA is an independent watchdog that regulates the content of advertisements, sales promotions and direct marketing in the UK.

How does the ASA protect consumers' interests?

- It investigates complaints about food advertisements.
- It monitors food advertisements.
- It takes action against misleading, harmful or offensive advertisements, sales promotions and direct marketing of food products.

What types of advertising do they deal with?

The types of ads they deal with include:

- magazine and newspaper advertisements

- radio and TV commercials (not programmes or programme sponsorship)

- television shopping channels

- advertisements on the internet

- posters on legitimate poster sites

- leaflets and brochures

- cinema commercials

- direct mail (advertising sent through the post and addressed to you personally).

> ⚠ **Watch point**
>
> Advertisements, wherever they appear must be **legal**, **decent**, **honest** and **truthful**.

Trading Standards

www.tradingstandards.gov.uk/

This government department looks after the interests of consumers and traders by enforcing fair trading laws and investigating consumer complaints.

How does Trading Standards protect consumers' interests?

Trading Standards officers will check:

- Factories, shops, pubs and markets for accurate weights and measures in food products and drinks.

- Advertisements or descriptions of products to make sure they are accurately described.

- Food labelling is accurate with regard to the composition of the product.

- Traders do not falsely describe either by word or in writing any products or services they are selling.

Where do I find Trading Standards?

Use the internet or look up a phone book for the nearest office.

Which?

www.which.co.uk/

A non-profit making organisation that works to make things better for the consumer. Used to be known as the Consumers Association.

How does Which? protect consumers' interests?

- They offer information and advice to help consumers make more informed decisions about food and health-related topics.

- They test food products, appliances, food services, etc. each year and publish the results in their magazines and on www.which.co.uk.

- By carrying out investigations into a range of services linked to the food industry, e.g. comparing supermarkets and food products and then awarding '**Best Buy**' and '**Recommended**' to products to help consumers make choices.

Citizens Advice Bureau

The service provides free, independent and confidential advice to everyone on their rights and responsibilities.

How does the Citizens Advice Bureau protect consumers' interests?

If you have a problem, the Citizens Advice Bureau will give you advice on the next steps to take. For example, if you had a complaint about:

- a restaurant's food hygiene, they would refer you to the Environmental Health Department

- a product not being accurately weighed in a shop, they would refer you to Trading Standards.

🔍 Hint

Which? is only one way of gaining information about goods and services. Visiting the internet can also lead you to a range of sites that can give you information and comparisons.

✔ Test your knowledge

1. What does the abbreviation ASA stand for?
2. State the type of advertising the ASA deal with.
3. What are the three rights of consumers?
4. Describe the role of a Trading Standards Officer.

Topic 2: Environmental Health Department, Food Standards Agency

Environmental Health Department (EHD)

The Environmental Health Department (EHD) employs Environmental Health Officers (EHOs) who protect the interests of the consumer.

What will the EHD want to know?
If the consumer has:

- bought or been served food that:

  - was unfit to eat
  - has been damaged by pests or
  - contained items it shouldn't have

- bought or been offered food that was past its 'use-by' date

- has seen bad hygiene practices in a food shop or restaurant

- been ill after eating out.

How does EHOs protect consumers' interests?
They will:

- Investigate consumer complaints of poor hygiene or other problems with food businesses.

- Investigate consumer complaints of unsatisfactory food or food that is unfit for human consumption.

- Inspect local food businesses to check that food hygiene regulations are being followed, by:

  - entering food premises on a routine check or to investigate complaints
  - identifying potential hazards in the food chain and carrying out risk assessment
  - inspecting food to see if it is safe and retain, seize or condemn food that isn't
  - taking away food samples to be tested and make videos to record what they see
  - giving food businesses time to carry out any improvements needed
  - immediately closing down any food premises that are a major threat to consumers' health.

- Provide advice for businesses and consumers on good food hygiene and on complying with the legal standards for food safety.

Make the link
Refer to Chapter 6.

Food Standards Agency (FSA)
www.food.gov.uk

An independent government department responsible for food safety and hygiene across the UK. The Agency regularly consults with consumers to understand their views and concerns about food-related issues.

You can access food hygiene ratings on the move. Download the app.

How does the FSA protect consumers' interests?
They:

- give advice about the nutrient content of foods and dietary issues

- help people to eat more healthily by providing information on healthy eating matters

- help promote accurate and clear food labelling, helping consumers make informed choices

- improve food safety throughout the food chain, reducing the risk to consumers

- agree licensing of meat processing companies and for hygiene controls on meat and meat products

- control genetically modified food

- monitor the use of food additives.

The FSA helps to educate consumers through leaflets, posters and a website which has online experts on nutrition and health to answer queries.

☑ Test your knowledge

1. Explain the role of an Environmental Health Officer in protecting the consumer.
2. What is the responsibility of the Food Standards Agency?
3. How does the Food Standards Agency help to educate consumers?

Let's cook

Working in pairs

Make a recipe where one person plays the chef (i.e. cooks the dish) and the other person plays the EHO (Environmental Health Officer) who notes down any positive and negative hygiene practices observed.

At the end of making the dish the EHO should give the chef feedback on his or her performance in the kitchen.

If time allows, swap roles and repeat the task with a different recipe.

GO! End of chapter activities

On your own

Case study 1

You and your family had a meal in a restaurant to celebrate your birthday.
The next day you all suffer from sickness and diarrhoea.

Which consumer organisation protects your interests?

What action should they take?

Case study 2

You have bought 2kg of bananas from the local market. You weigh them when you get home and discover you have only been given 1.5kg.

Which consumer organisation protects your interests?

What action should they take?

Case study 3

When you were at an outdoor rock festival you noticed that the people selling burgers were smoking and coughing over the food.

Which consumer organisation protects your interests?

What action should they take?

Case study 4

You have bought a loaf of freshly made bread from the local supermarket. When you cut it open you find a dead fly.

Which consumer organisation protects your interests?

What action should they take?

Do this task well as it could be kept for your portfolio of work.

? Exam-style questions

To help you prepare for the exam, remember to look at pages 191–202, Keeping on track: preparing for the National 5 course assessment.

Question 1

State **two** reasons why each of the following would inspect food premises:

i Environmental Health Officer **2 marks**

ii Trading Standards Officer. **2 marks**

Question 2

Describe **one** way the Advertising Standards Authority (ASA)
protects consumers' interests. **1 mark**

Question 3

Explain **one** way the Citizens Advice Bureau protects consumers' interests. **1 mark**

Question 4

Describe **two** ways the Food Standards Agency protects consumers' interests. **2 marks**

Now check your answers at the back of the book.

Rate your progress

How confident are you that you have achieved each of the following objectives?

Using the following key as a guide, give yourself a rating for each of the objectives below

Rating	Explanation
1	Confident with the standard of my work
2	Fairly confident with the standard of my work
3	The majority of my work was satisfactory
4	Require to do some further work
5	Require a lot of work

Objectives	Rating
Describe how the following organisations protect the interests of consumers:	
Advertising Standards Authority	
Trading Standards	
Which?	
Citizens Advice Bureau	
Environmental Health Department	
Food Standards Agency	

Look at your ratings.

Write down two **next steps** to 'unlocking' your knowledge of contemporary food issues.

12 Food labelling and the consumer

Topic 1: Statutory/voluntary food labelling

Food labelling can be either:

- **Statutory** – compulsory information that has to be on the label by law.

- **Voluntary** – this information is supplied voluntarily by manufacturers to give consumers a little more information about the product.

Statutory food labelling requirements

Food labelling must follow the current food labelling regulations.

Food labels will:

- give you accurate information about the food product so you know what you are buying

- help you to make informed dietary choices

- help you to choose between different foods, brands and flavours.

> ⚠ **Watch point**
>
> Keep up to date with labelling by looking at the Food Standards Agency website.

How are these food labels going to help me?

How are consumers' food choices affected by labelling?

The food label **must** by law show the following **statutory** information.

Statutory information	How this could affect consumers' food choices
The name of the food and/or a description of what the product is	• Consumers will know exactly what the food is. • They can take account of likes and dislikes. • It will inform them if the food has been processed in any way, e.g. condensed milk.
A list of ingredients in weight order (biggest first). Certain food allergens and additives must be included	• The consumer will know exactly all the ingredients in the product and their proportions. • For people with allergies, the ingredients will list nuts, milk, egg, fish, gluten so these products can be avoided. • Some consumers may be allergic to certain additives and need to know if they are present in a food. • Certain ingredients may need to be avoided for religious reasons or because the person may be a vegetarian.
Date marking 'Use by' or 'Best before' are required by law	• These give information on how to store the foods properly and safely. • They let the consumer know when the food should be eaten by, reducing the risk of food poisoning. **Use by** Used on highly perishable foods, e.g. yoghurt, chicken. These foods will become a food poisoning risk if eaten after the stated date. Cook or freeze any foods before the 'use by' date to prevent wastage. Check the packaging to make sure the food can be frozen as sometimes foods have been pre-frozen, especially shellfish. **Best before** The best before date is the date up to which the manufacturers expect food to remain at peak quality if stored correctly. It is used on food like pasta, flour, biscuits, tinned and dried foods which have a longer shelf-life. They may not be 'at their best', e.g. biscuits may have gone a bit soft, but these foods will not cause food poisoning.
Name and address of manufacturer, packer or EU seller	• Consumers may be more inclined to buy products from manufacturers who have a good reputation for quality. • May be needed in case of complaint.
Weight or **volume** of product	• Helps the consumer to work out value for money and compare products. • A lot of pre-packed goods carry the 'e' mark. This means that the average quantity must be accurate but the weight of each pack may vary slightly.
Place of origin/where it comes from	• Some consumers may not buy products from certain countries on moral or political grounds.
Storage instructions	• This tells the consumer how and where to store the food to ensure it remains safe to eat and at its best.
Instructions for use/cooking	• Helps to ensure that foods are correctly prepared and cooked to prevent food poisoning. • Lets consumers know if they have the time, skills and equipment to prepare the food.

Voluntary food labelling

Voluntary labelling is additional information such as nutritional figures, bar codes, customer-care and environmental information. This helps the consumer to make more informed choices, e.g. choosing food to meet dietary requirements or choosing foods which have packaging that can be recycled. Manufacturers use it as a way of promoting their product.

What's the reason for voluntary labelling?

Nutritional information

Many food labels show nutritional information, however food companies do not have to provide this information unless they are making a claim about their product such as 'low sugar' or 'low fat'.

The nutritional information usually gives the proportion of protein, fat, carbohydrate, vitamins and minerals and the energy values. Some labels give a further breakdown of these groups such as the different types of carbohydrates and fats. They also give information about the sodium (salt) and fibre content.

Guideline daily amounts (GDAs)

Guideline daily amounts or GDAs are a guide to what people can consume each day for a healthy, balanced diet.

The GDA label shows the number of calories and amount of sugars, fat, saturates (saturated fat) and salt per portion of food in grams. This is also expressed as a percentage of your guideline daily amount.

Traffic-light labelling

As an alternative to the GDA label and to make food labelling simpler and easier to read at a glance, the Food Standards Agency has approved traffic light labels which indicate whether food has high (red), medium (amber) or low (green) amounts of fat, saturated fat, sugars and salt.

In addition to traffic light colours the number of grams of fat, saturated fat, sugars and salt are indicated for a typical serving of the food.

Manufacturers have agreed on the value of traffic light labelling and are looking to include it on their packaging.

Barcodes

A barcode is a label printed on packages which identifies goods in a form which can be read electronically and transmitted to a computer. Computerised checkouts read the barcodes and the scanner sends the information to an in-store computer.

> **⚠ Watch point**
>
> Nutritional labelling will become mandatory in 2016. Check the Food Standards Agency website for information.

> **:: Make the link**
>
> Refer to Chapter 11, Trading Standards.

Why are barcodes useful to the consumer?

- They speed up payment at the point of sale.

- Less chance of being wrongly charged.

- Better stock control for the supermarket.

- Consumers can self-scan products at the checkout.

Customer care

Microwave labelling scheme

Microwaves vary in their ability to reheat food so a labelling system was introduced to ensure people using different ovens cooked foods properly. This also ensures foods are heated thoroughly to reduce the risk of food poisoning.

The **microwave symbol** shows the oven has been labelled in compliance with the scheme.

The **power output** box shows the power output in watts. The higher the number, the faster the food will be heated and the shorter the cooking time.

Indicates the oven is a 'microwave oven'

Power output

800W

F

Heating category

The **heating category** box shows a letter. This is the heating category based on the oven's ability to heat small food packs.

Vegetarian labels

At present there is no single legal definition of the terms 'vegetarian' or 'vegan' either at European or the UK level, and the 'Suitable for Vegetarians' logo is voluntary and not regulated.

However, such voluntary claims are subject to the general controls in the EU food labelling directive which are reflected in the UK's Food Safety Act 1990.

Products that carry the **Vegetarian Society Approved** logo, known as the Seedling Symbol, must fulfil certain requirements laid down by the society.

- Products have to be free of animal flesh or any other products resulting from slaughter, e.g. meat or bone stock.

- Products and ingredients should not have been tested on animals.

- Eggs must be free range.

- Products must be GM free.

- Products must not have come in contact with any non-vegetarian products/ingredients during production.

Own-brand labelling

Some supermarkets have their own labels/logos to indicate if the product:

- is suitable for freezing

- is suitable for vegetarians

- offers allergy advice

- highlights fortification of food products

- promotes current dietary advice.

> ⚠ **Watch point**
>
> Some supermarkets have their own labelling logos/symbols for vegetarian products, however these products may not be suitable for vegans – read the ingredients list carefully.
>
> Other voluntary labelling includes whether the product is organic and if the packaging material is recyclable. (Refer to Chapter 9 for more information.)

✔ Test your knowledge

1. Explain the difference between voluntary and statutory labelling.

2. List four voluntary pieces of information that could be on a food label and explain the benefit of each to the consumer.

3. Explain the difference between GDA and traffic-light labelling.

4. Explain in detail the following label:

🍲 Let's cook

Lesson 1
Prepare a home-made tomato and basil sauce for a cook-chill range. Develop a label to show how to store it.

Lesson 2
Use the sauce for a chicken parmesan bake – use Quorn™ for a vegetarian option.

Lesson 3
Make up an ingredients list for the dish that could be included on the packaging.

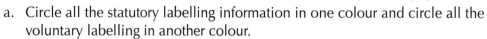 End of chapter activities

Activity 1

Working in pairs

Study the labels of a range of food products and make a list of all the nutrients commonly found on the labels.

Activity 2

On your own

Take an item of packaging, open it out and glue it to an A3 piece of paper.

a. Circle all the statutory labelling information in one colour and circle all the voluntary labelling in another colour.

b. Select four pieces of information and explain how each piece of information helps consumers make informed choices.

Do this task well as it could be used for your portfolio of work.

Activity 3

On your own

Using the internet, look up **one** of the following topics and write a report about what you find.

- Public want food 'traffic lights'
- Label wars: GDA vs traffic light
- Foods Standards Agency: traffic-light labelling

As a class discuss your findings for each of the topics.

Activity 4

Set up two teams to debate GDA vs traffic-light labelling.

As a class discuss which one is most preferred and would be better for the consumer.

Activity 5

As a class, design a leaflet to inform consumers about voluntary and statutory labelling.

Activity 6

On your own

a. List four statutory pieces of information that must be on a food label.

b. Explain how each piece of information could affect a consumer's food choices.

Do this task well as it could be used for your portfolio of work.

? Exam-style questions

To help you prepare for the exam, remember to look at pages 191–202, Keeping on track: preparing for the National 5 course assessment.

Question 1

Identify **three** points of information which, by **law**, must be stated on a food label.

Explain the importance of **each** point to the consumer.

6 marks

Question 2

The following labels may be found on food packaging.

Give two reasons why **each** label is useful to the consumer.

a)
b)

4 marks

Question 3

Explain the importance to the consumer of **four** of the pieces of information found on the following food label for spicy potato cakes.

Hepburn's Spicy Potato Cakes	
Ingredients Potatoes, sweet potatoes, red chillies, onions, breadcrumbs, coriander, garlic puree, salt, vegetable oil. Breadcrumbs contain wheatflour, yeast, salt.	**Storage** Keep refrigerated. Not suitable for freezing.
Cooking instructions Preheat oven. Remove cakes from packaging. Place cakes on baking tray. 200 °C; Fan 170 °C; Gas 6 25 minutes in oven Check that the product is piping hot before serving. **Do not reheat.**	Use by **12 Jun** **450g** ℮

4 marks

Now check your answers at the back of the book.

Rate your progress

How confident are you that you have achieved each of the following objectives?

Using the following key as a guide, give yourself a rating for each of the objectives below

Rating	Explanation
1	Confident with the standard of my work
2	Fairly confident with the standard of my work
3	The majority of my work was satisfactory
4	Require to do some further work
5	Require a lot of work

Objectives	Rating
Explain the difference between statutory and voluntary labelling	
Explain how food labelling information can affect consumers' food choices	

Look at your ratings.

Write down two **next steps** to 'unlocking' your knowledge of food and health.

Keeping on track

Preparing for the National 5 course assessment

There are two components to the National 5 course assessment:

- **An assignment** to be submitted to SQA.
  This is worth 50 marks.

- **A question paper** marked by SQA and worth 50 marks.

There will be five questions in the question paper, each worth 10 marks. They will all start with a **short scenario** which gives **information** to help you answer the question.

> ⚠ **Watch point**
>
> It is important to **read the information in the scenario carefully** because each part of the question will link to this.

TOP TIPS FOR ANSWERING THE EXAM PAPER

1. Read the question **carefully**.

2. Highlight the **key words** of the question. Your answers should always **link** to the **key words**.

3. Make sure you answer **all** the questions.

4. If you get stuck with a question, **leave a space** and come **back to it later**.

5. **Read over** your answers when you have finished.

6. **Watch your time** – you have **1 hour 30 minutes** to complete the question paper.

Types of questions
There are **five** types of questions in the question paper.

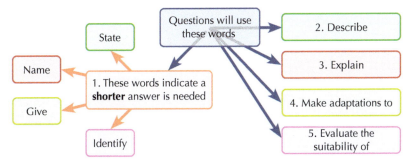

Some questions will use **one** of these words and some will use **a combination of two**, e.g. identify and explain.

Always look at:

1. The **number of marks** awarded to each part of the question.
2. The **space available** to write your answers.

These will give you a guide to the number and depth of answers required.

Below are examples of the type of question you might be asked and sample answers.

Part 1: questions which require short answers

> **State/Name/Identify/Give**
> This means you have to provide a **fact or a short statement** linked to the key words in the question.

> **State**

Examples

Question 1

For each of the following nutrients **state one** function and **one** food source.   **4 marks**

Sample answer

Nutrient: Calcium	
Function: Needed to make strong bones and teeth	**1 mark**
Food source: Milk	**1 mark**
Nutrient: Vitamin A	
Function: Helps vision in dim light	**1 mark**
Food source: Carrots	**1 mark**
	Total: **4 marks**

Question 2

State two reasons why a manufacturer would carry out market research when developing a new product.   **2 marks**

Sample answer

1.	To find out why sales of a product are falling	**1 mark**
2.	To find out what kind of product the consumer would like	**1 mark**
		Total: **2 marks**

Name

Example
Question 1

Name two food sources of **each** of the following types of carbohydrate:

  i. Total complex carbohydrate

  ii. Sugar   **4 marks**

Sample answer

  i. Total complex carbohydrate:

  Pasta   **1 mark**

  Bread   **1 mark**

  ii. Sugar

  Cakes   **1 mark**

  Biscuits   **1 mark**

                                                                                        Total: **4 marks**

Identify

Example
Question 1

Identify two steps a manufacturer might carry out in the food product development process.   **2 marks**

Sample answer

  i. Concept generation   **1 mark**

  ii. Launch   **1 mark**

                                                                                        Total: **2 marks**

Give (Give reasons for...)

Examples

Question 1

Give two factors that could affect a consumer's choice of food.   **2 marks**

Sample answer

i.	Budget available	**1 mark**
ii.	Adverts on television	**1 mark**
		Total: **2 marks**

Question 2

Competitors at a sports event want to buy **healthy food**. A catering van at the event is offering the following three meal deals.

Study the following information about the meal deals and **state** the **most suitable** for the competitors to buy.

Meal deal A	Meal deal B	Meal deal C
Cheese and pickle in a white roll	Egg mayonnaise in a seeded baguette	Chicken and salad in a wholemeal wrap
Packet of crisps	Chocolate chip muffin	An apple
Carton of orange juice	Can of cola	Bottle of water

3 marks

Sample answer

State the most suitable meal deal for the competitors:

Meal deal C   **1 mark**

Give three reasons for your choice:

Reason 1: The wrap is a source of fibre and is filling for the competitors.   **1 mark**

Reason 2: The chicken is lower in fat, helping the competitors to reduce the fat in their diet. **1 mark**

Reason 3: The apple will help the competitors meet the dietary target for fruit
          and vegetables.   **1 mark**

Total: **4 marks**

⚠ Watch point

The three reasons must justify your choice.

Part 2: questions which require more information in the answers

Describe
This means you have to provide straightforward **points of information** linked to the key words in the question.

Explain
This means you have to provide more detailed points of information linked to the key words in the question. This could include, e.g.

* giving reasons for
* explaining the effects of.

> ⚠ **Watch point**
> Remember **BATS** – 'Because', 'As', 'Therefore' or 'So'. Using these words will help you give more detail in your answers.

Question 1

Describe what happens to vitamin C in vegetables during each of the following:

   i. Left to soak in water.

   ii. Prepared two hours before cooking.   **2 marks**

Sample answer

i. The vitamin C leaches into the water	**1 mark**
ii. The vitamin C oxidises into the air	**1 mark**
	Total: **2 marks**

Question 2

Explain two ways in which a consumer's choice of food could be affected by their budget.   **2 marks**

Sample answer

Explanation 1: If the budget is limited, consumers may choose more shop's own economy brands, as they will be cheaper.	**1 mark**
Explanation 2: If a consumer has more money to spend, they may buy better quality luxury foods.	**1 mark**
	Total: **2 marks**

Question 3

This question asks you to both **describe** and **explain**.

The takeaway sandwich bar in school would like to make a <mark>healthier</mark> version of their chicken pitta bread, which is popular with pupils.

> **Chicken pitta bread**
> White pitta bread
> Fried chicken strips
> Mayonnaise
> Grated cheddar cheese
> Salt

Describe three <mark>changes</mark> they could make to the chicken pitta bread and **explain** how each change helps to meet a **different** piece of <mark>current dietary advice</mark>. **6 marks**

Sample answer

Change 1: Grill the chicken instead of frying.	**1 mark**
Explanation: The fat would run off during grilling so this would reduce the fat content.	**1 mark**
Change 2: Add salad to the pitta bread.	**1 mark**
Explanation: This would help increase fruit and vegetable intake to 400g per day.	**1 mark**
Change 3: Replace the white pitta bread with wholemeal pitta.	**1 mark**
Explanation: This would increase the fibre content of the pitta bread.	**1 mark**
	Total: **6 marks**

> **State/Identify/State/Explain**
> This question will have to be answered in two stages.
> **Stage 1** – you have to **list** the facts.
> **Stage 2** – link the **explanation** to the fact(s) and key words.

Question 1

Name **two** <mark>nutrients</mark> found in <mark>meat</mark> and explain at least **one** <mark>function</mark> of **each** in the diet.

4 marks

Sample answer

1. Nutrient: protein	**1 mark**
Function: needed for growth and repair of body cells	**1 mark**
2. Nutrient: iron	**1 mark**
Function: helps to make red blood cells so preventing anaemia	**1 mark**
	Total: **4 marks**

Question 2

Identify and **explain two** factors linked to diet which may contribute to
obesity in children.   **4 marks**

Sample answer

Identify: High intake of fast foods	**1 mark**
Explanation: as these are often high in fat and they may increase the risk of obesity in children.	**1 mark**
Identify: High intake of sugary drinks and sweets	**1 mark**
Explanation: if children are not active they are more at risk of obesity as these foods are high in energy/calories.	**1 mark**
	Total: **4 marks**

Question 3

A health conscious student wishes to buy a ready meal.

Identify the **most suitable** meal from the three shown below.

 Hint

Read over the information in the table carefully. Compare the figures for energy, nutrients and fibre for each meal and highlight (or underline or ✓) the figures that are the most suitable for a health conscious student. This will help you to decide which ready meal to choose.

Information about ready meals							
	Energy (kJ)	Protein (g)	Fat (g)	Of which saturates (g)	Sodium (g)	Iron (mg)	fibre (g)
Meal A	2·910	16·0	15·3	12·0	1·2	6·0	7·9
Meal B	1·608	17·5	8·7	2·2	0·5	5·9	9·8
Meal C	1·883	15·4	9·8	5·2	0·6	3·7	4·9

Sample answer

Identify the most suitable ready meal for the student:

Ready meal B	**1 mark**

Explain **three** reasons for your choice.

1. The salt in this ready meal is the lowest, so will reduce the risk
   of the student developing high blood pressure later in life.   **1 mark**

2. This ready meal is the lowest in energy so will help prevent the
   student becoming overweight.   **1 mark**

3. The iron is the second highest so will reduce the risk of the
   student becoming anaemic.   **1 mark**

Hint

Note that although the iron was not highlighted, there was only
0.1g of difference between Meal A and B, which is not a lot.

Make adapatations to
This means you have to make changes to improve the recipe or dish given in the question.

Question 1

A café wishes to adapt the following recipe to meet current dietary advice.

> **Pasta surprise**
> Pasta twists
> Butter
> Flour
> Whole milk
> Cheddar cheese
> Salt

Identify two adaptations that could be made to the recipe and explain how each adaptation
helps meet a **different** piece of current dietary advice.

Sample answers

Adaptation: Change the pasta to wholegrain pasta	**1 mark**
Explanation: Wholegrain pasta contains more fibre, which would help meet the dietary goal of increasing dietary fibre.	**1 mark**
Adaptation: Add salmon to the dish	**1 mark**
Explanation: as the intake of oily fish should increase to one portion per week and this would be one way of adding it.	**1 mark**
	Total: **4 marks**

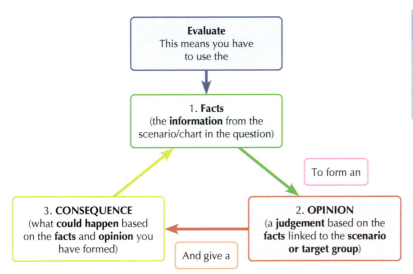

🔍 Hint

Remember **BATS** – 'Because', 'As', 'Therefore' or 'So'. Using these words will help you give more detail in your answers.

This is **one method** of answering this type of question – there are other methods. **It is important to use your subject knowledge to make a judgement based on the information in the question**.

In the question paper you will always get an evaluation question about Dietary Reference Values **linked** to the person in the case study.

🔍 Hint

It may be a good idea to include the words 'so' or 'as' to help you with your consequence.

1. Highlight the key words in the question.

2. Carefully read all of the **facts** first.

This is where you must compare the figures for **Dietary Reference Values** against those in the **Dietary Analysis** chart for the person in the case study.

You could also put + (if it is **more/high**) or – (if it is **less/low**) beside each of the figures.

3. Where there is a small difference you could place a ✓ beside the figures. This shows it is just about the right amount.

4. Using either the **+**, ✓ or –, form an **opinion** as to whether the energy/nutrients/fibre are **too high**, about the **right amount** or **too low** for the person in the case study.

🔍 Hint

There is more than one type of evaluation question.

5. Write a **consequence** linked to the **facts** in the scenario and your **opinion**.

Question 1

An active two-year-old toddler has fallen at nursery and broken her arm.

 Hint

The key to success in this type of question is to know the function of nutrients and how they affect health.

Dietary Reference Values for a girl aged 1–3 years					
Estimated Average Requirements	Reference Nutrient Intake				
Energy (MJ)	Protein (g)	Calcium (mg)	Vitamin B1 mg	Iron (mg)	Vitamin C (mg)
5·20	14·5	350	0·5	6·9	30

The table below shows the dietary analysis of a day's meals for the two-year-old toddler. Remember to compare the DRV chart and the figures below and insert a **+**, **✓** or **–**.

Dietary Analysis of the toddler's meals					
Energy (MJ)	Protein (g)	Calcium (mg	Vitamin B1 mg	Iron(mg)	Vitamin C (mg)
6·10 +	11·8 −	380 +	0·6 ✓	4·2 −	35 +

Taking account of the Dietary Reference Values (DRVs) for a girl aged 1–3 years, **evaluate** the suitability of the toddler's meals.

> ⚠ **Watch point**
>
> Each answer is awarded 1 mark in the question paper.
>
> For this style of question, a **maximum of 4 marks** can be awarded for **evaluations** linked to **four different** aspects of the day's meals for the toddler.
>
> To gain the **other 2 marks** you must **develop two of these aspects** further.

Sample answer

Evaluation

Point 1
The amount of protein is lower than required **[facts]** for the toddler so there is not
enough **[opinion]** so will affect how well her broken arm repairs **[consequence]**.   **1 mark**

Point 2
The amount of calcium is higher than is needed **[facts]** which is good **[opinion]**
as it will help the toddler's broken bone to heal **[consequence]**.   **1 mark**

Point 3
The vitamin C content is high **[facts]** so this is suitable for the toddler **[opinion]**
as it will help the iron to be absorbed **[consequence]**.   **1 mark**

Point 4
Because she has enough vitamin C, this reduces the risk of anaemia **[second
consequence linked to facts and opinion already given in point 3]**.

1 mark for developed evaluation of point 3

Point 5
She is only getting 4.2mg of iron **[facts]**, this is lower than she should have **[opinion]**
and means the toddler may become tired **[consequence]**.   **1 mark**

Point 6
Because she is lacking in iron, she may be more at risk of becoming anaemic
[second answer is developed – linked to facts and opinion already given in point 5].

1 mark for developed evaluation of point 5
Total: **6 marks**

 Watch point

Another way to gain 6 marks is:

3 marks can be awarded for **evaluations** linked to **three different**
aspects of the day's meals for the toddler. To gain the **other 3
marks** you must **further develop each of these three aspects**.

Question 2

A fourth year pupil often sleeps late and does not have time for breakfast before leaving home.
Evaluate the suitability of the breakfast bar for a teenager to eat on the way to school.

No added sugar
Pack contains four individually wrapped bars
Eat straight from the packet
No refrigeration required
Varieties available: cranberry, mango
Contains no artificial colours and flavours

Sample answers

Point 1
There are only fruit flavours available **[facts]** which might not be suitable if
she does not like the taste of fruit **[opinion]**. If the teenager doesn't like fruit,
she will not want to eat them **[consequence]**.   **1 mark**

Point 2
It contains no artificial colours and flavours **[facts]** so it is suitable for the
teenager **[opinion]** as it reduces the risk of any allergic reactions **[consequence]**.   **1 mark**

Point 3
No refrigeration is needed **[facts]** so it is suitable for the teenager **[opinion]**
as it can be kept until she is hungry **[consequence]**.   **1 mark**

Point 4
As it does not need refrigeration this will reduce the risk of her getting
food poisoning. **[Second answer is developed – linked to facts and opinion
already given in point 3.]**

1 mark for developed evaluation point
Total: **4 marks**

⚠ Watch point

To gain 4 marks:
- **four** evaluative comments **each** linked to a **different aspect** of
  the breakfast bar **or**
- **two** evaluative comments linked to **each of two different aspects**
  of the breakfast bar

Or
- **two** evaluative comments **each linked to a different aspect** of the
  breakfast bar
- **+ two** evaluative comments **linked to a third aspect** of the
  breakfast bar (as shown above)

Finally, always make sure your answers give enough relevant information.

Answers

Unit 1: Food for Health

Chapter 1

Question 1

Nutrient	Function
Carbohydrate	• To supply energy for all activities. • To supply warmth and so help maintain normal body temperature. • Can act as a protein sparer.
Protein	• Growth and repair of body cells. • Maintenance of body cells and tissues. • Secondary source of energy.
Vitamin B complex	• Helps release energy from food so people do not feel tired. • Required for the function of the nervous system. • Needed to help normal growth in children.
Calcium	• Combines to make calcium phosphate which gives hardness and strength to bones and teeth. • Required for the maintenance of bones and teeth. • Helps to prevent osteoporosis in later life. • Helps blood to clot after injury. • Required for the correct functioning of muscles and nerves.
Iron	• Needed for making red blood cells. • Prevents anaemia.

2 × 1 mark for nutrients; 2 × 1 mark for function; Total: 4 marks

Question 2
1. Vitamin D works with calcium to aid absorption and form strong bones and teeth.
2. Without vitamin D the body cannot make use of the calcium in food.
3. Without vitamin D less calcium will be absorbed and this will affect the strength of bones and teeth.

Any one answer for 1 mark

Question 3

Storing vegetables	Preparing vegetables	Cooking vegetables
1. Store in a cool dark place/ away from light. 2. Store in salad drawer of refrigerator. 3. Store for as short a time as possible.	1. Do not peel/peel very thinly. 2. Prepare just before needed. 3. Do not soak in water. 4. Use a sharp knife. 5. Do not chop into small pieces/use as large as possible.	1. Cook vegetables for as short a time as possible. 2. Cook in as little water as possible. 3. Cook with the lid on/in a covered container. 4. Steam/microwave. 5. Use vegetable water for soups/ sauces (to recycle vitamin C). 6. Do not keep warm/reheat.

1 mark from each area; Total: 3 marks

Question 4

Functions	Practical ways
1. Essential for maintaining the correct fluid balance in the body. 2. Required for correct muscle and nerve activity. 3. Prevents muscle cramps.	1. Replace ready-made foods with home-made versions. 2. Limit intake of processed foods (e.g. ham/cheese). 3. Limit intake of salty snacks (e.g. crisps). 4. Replace salt with LoSalt/salt substitute. 5. Use herbs/spices to flavour food. 6. Read labels and choose lower salt products. 7. Taste food before adding salt.

2 × 1 mark for functions; 2 × 1 mark for practical ways; Total: 4 marks

Chapter 2

Question 1

1. Replace (whole) milk with semi-skimmed/skimmed milk.
2. Replace butter/margarine with low-fat spread.
3. Choose cottage/Edam/reduced-fat cheese to replace cheddar/hard cheese.
4. Choose lean meat/cut any extra fat from meat/replace red meat with white meat.
5. Replace high-fat snacks (e.g. crisps) with, e.g. bread products/fruit.
6. Grill/bake/steam/poach/microwave foods instead of frying.
7. Skim fat from gravy/soups/stews.
8. When frying use a griddle-pan/dry fry.
9. Read labels and choose lower-fat products.
10. Use reduced-fat versions of products.

2 × 1 mark; Total: 2 marks

Question 2

Adaptation	How dietary advice is met
1. Add other vegetables to the dish (any other suitable vegetable would be acceptable). 2. Increase proportion of tomatoes in the dish.	This would contribute to increasing the average intake of a variety of fruit and vegetables to at least five portions or 400g per day.
1. Add (wholemeal) breadcrumbs as a topping to the dish. 2. Incorporate breadcrumbs in the sauce. 3. Add crushed wholegrain breakfast cereal as a topping to the dish. 4. Use wholemeal flour instead of white flour.	This would contribute to increasing the average intake of fibre to 18g per day.
1. Change butter to low-fat alternative. 2. Change milk to skimmed or semi-skimmed milk.	This would help to reduce the average total fat intake to no more than 35% of food energy. This would help to reduce the average saturated fat intake to no more than 11% of food energy.

Adaptation	How dietary advice is met
1. Remove salt from dish. 2. Replace salt with herbs/LoSalt (for flavouring). 3. Reduce proportion of salt in dish.	This would help reduce the average intake of salt to 6g per day (approx. 1 tsp.)
1. Use sliced potatoes with skins on as a topping for the dish. 2. Include wholegrain pasta in the dish. 3. Include a serving of wholegrain rice with the dish.	This would contribute to increasing the average intake of fibre to 18g per day. It may also contribute to a reduction in calorie intake, as it is replacing high fat foods with complex carbohydrates such as wholegrain rice and potatoes.
1. Change haddock to an oily fish (any suitable oily fish would be acceptable).	This would help to increase the consumption of oily fish to one 140g portion per week.

Adaptation: **3 × 1 mark**; Meeting current dietary advice: **3 × 1 mark**; Total: **6 marks**

Question 3

1. Use bread to accompany soups/main courses.
2. Use bread in dessert, e.g. bread and butter/summer pudding.
3. Serve sandwiches to replace high fat/sugar snacks.
4. Use breadcrumbs to top savoury dishes/coat foods for frying.
5. Breadcrumbs can be added to provide bulk, e.g. burgers.

2 × 1 marks; Total: **2 marks**

Chapter 3

Question 1

Fact	Opinion	Consequence
Energy: 7·36 MJ Low in energy Provides less energy Slightly low in energy	Not suitable/bad May be suitable	1. May not have enough energy for physical activity/all body activity throughout the day. 2. May become tired and lose concentration. 3. May not do much exercise to use up more energy, therefore she will be less likely to become overweight.
NSP: 14·2 g Low in fibre/less than she needs	Not suitable/bad	1. Could contribute to an increased risk of bowel cancer/diverticulitis in later life. 2. This could increase her risk of constipation. 3. Foods high in NSP are filling/help control body weight, therefore she will be at greater risk of obesity/weight gain.
Vitamin B1: 0·85 mg Just about the right amount	Suitable/good	1. So there is enough for the release of energy from food to allow her to work/be active. 2. Will help her maintain her muscle tone as she may be concerned about her appearance. 3. As vitamin B is not stored in the body and has to be replaced daily.

Fact	Opinion	Consequence
Vitamin C: 30 mg Low in vitamin C	Not suitable	1. Her anaemia may become worse. 2. She may pick up infections more easily. 3. If she injures herself then it will take longer for the injury to heal. 4. She may be more likely to develop cancer/heart disease in later life as vitamin C is an antioxidant vitamin.
Iron: 16·9 mg	Suitable	1. If this intake continued, it would help her anaemia. 2. She is less likely to feel tired/faint.
Sodium: 1800 mg	Not suitable	1. May increase her risk of high blood pressure/hypertension in later life. 2. May increase her risk of stroke/heart disease in later life.

Either:

- **four** evaluative comments, **each** linked to a **different aspect** of the girl's meals (maximum of 4 marks) and **two** additional evaluative answers linked to two of the aspects identified (**2 marks**) or
- **two** evaluative comments linked to **each of three different aspects** of the girl's meals (3 × 2 marks) or
- **two** evaluative comments **each linked to two different aspects** of the girl's meals (2 × 2 marks) + **two** evaluative answers **linked to two further aspects** of the girl's meals (2 marks).

Total: **6 marks**

Question 2
Snack B

Most suitable snack – snack B

	Reason
Energy: 716kJ/169 kcals/ lowest	Lowest in energy so the toddler is less likely to become overweight/obese. So the toddler will probably use this up/little excess energy to be stored as fat. Will help give the toddler energy to last until next meal. The toddler is likely to be active.
Protein: 2·9g/highest	The toddler will need protein for growth as he/she is still growing. The toddler will need protein for repair of body tissues if he/she falls and hurts himself/herself. The toddler can use protein as an additional source of energy/if he/she is active.
Total fat: 1·1g/lowest **Saturates: 0·3g/lowest**	The toddler is less likely to suffer from obesity. The toddler is less likely to suffer from CHD in later life. Contributes to the target to reduce fat intake and the parent is keen for the toddler to have a healthy snack.

	Reason
Sugar: 1·5g/lowest	It will be less likely to rot the toddler's teeth.
	Will not taste too sweet, making the toddler less likely to develop a sweet tooth.
	Contributes to the dietary target to reduce sugar, and the parent is keen for the toddler to have a healthy snack.
	Will be less likely to contribute to Type 2 diabetes.
Salt: 0·17g/lowest	The toddler is less likely to suffer from high blood pressure/hypertension.
	Contributes to the dietary target to reduce salt and the parent is keen for the toddler to have a healthy snack.
	Toddler is less likely to develop a liking for salty foods.

Correct choice: **1 mark**; Reasons: **3 × 1 mark**; Total: **4 marks**

Chapter 4
Question 1

High blood pressure	Osteoporosis
1. Reduce salt/sodium intake.	1. Increase calcium intake.
2. Maintain healthy weight/avoid overweight/ obesity.	2. Increase vitamin D intake.
3. Reduce stress.	3. Maintain healthy weight/avoid overweight/ obesity.
4. Moderate intake of alcohol.	4. Exercise regularly/weight-bearing exercise.
5. Do not smoke.	5. Do not smoke.
6. Take regular exercise.	6. Moderate intake of alcohol.

2 × 2 marks each answer; Total: **4 marks**

Question 2

a) Eating too many sugary foods or drinks.
Eating too many fatty foods.
Increase in eating out/fast foods/takeaways/ready meals, which can be high in fat/sugar.
Obese parents may increase risk of obesity in their children.
Low income may lead to more high-fat/high-sugar foods and less fruit and vegetables being eaten.
Advertising can persuade consumers to choose sugary/fatty foods.
Lack of exercise or activity.
Increase in 'sedentary' pastimes, e.g. computer games/TV, using less energy.

2 × 1 mark

b) (Coronary) heart disease
Hypertension/high blood pressure
Diabetes
Osteoporosis

2 × 1 mark; Total: **4 marks**

ANSWERS

Question 3

Factors	Explanation
High sugar intake	Sweets and drinks with high quantities of sugar will contribute to obesity and HBP and so increase the risk of **CHD**. Type 2 diabetes can be caused as a result of obesity and this increases the risk of **CHD**.
High total or saturated fat intake	Cholesterol may form on artery walls, which will increase the risk of **CHD**.
Too few polyunsaturated fats	Omega-3, an essential fatty acid, is thought to help prevent cholesterol building up in the blood, which reduces the risk of **CHD**.
High salt intake	Raises blood pressure, which can lead to HBP and **CHD**.
Lack of fruit and vegetables	Fruit and vegetables are good sources of antioxidant vitamins, which help prevent **CHD**.
Diet low in fibre	Fibre will help reduce the amount of cholesterol in the blood so reduce the risk of **CHD**.
Lack of physical exercise	Lack of (physical) exercise can lead to obesity, increasing the risk of **CHD**.
Cigarette smoking	Smoking increases blood pressure, which is a risk factor in **CHD**.
Obesity	Obesity can raise blood pressure, which increases the risk of **CHD**.
Heredity	If there is a family history of heart disease then an individual may have an increased risk of **CHD** (as it may be passed on by the parents).
Alcohol	Too much alcohol can lead to high blood pressure/strain on the heart increasing the risk of **CHD**.

Identify: **2 × 1 mark**; Explanation: **2 × 1 mark**; Total: 4 **marks**

Question 4

Fact	Opinion	Consequence
Energy: 13·20MJ/13200kj Too much energy	Not suitable	1. Any extra energy could be converted to fat, making her more overweight. 2. Any extra energy could be converted to fat so further increasing her blood pressure. 3. Any extra energy could be converted to fat so increasing her risk of CHD/stroke. 4. She has a sedentary occupation and is unlikely to burn off the excess energy.
Protein: 48·0mg Slightly over	Suitable Not suitable	1. She will get enough protein for repair and maintenance of body tissues. 2. As there is likely to be extra protein which could be converted to energy and may contribute to her weight problem.

208

Fact	Opinion	Consequence
Vitamin B: 1·2mg Slightly over	Suitable	1. As there is enough for the release of energy (from food) to allow her to work.
Iron: 4·8mg Low/ less than is needed	Not suitable	1. She will/may feel tired at work. 2. She may feel tired/she may feel less likely to exercise and so lose weight. 3. She will be more likely to suffer from anaemia.
Sodium: 2·1g high	Not suitable	1. Further increases her blood pressure, which will increase her risk of a stroke/CHD.
Fibre: 12g	Not suitable	1. May feel hungry and could snack on high fat/sugar foods further increasing her weight. 2. May increase her risk of CHD/constipation/bowel disease.

Either:

- **four** evaluative comments **each** linked to a **different aspect** of the woman's meals (**maximum of 4 marks**) and **two further developed** evaluative comments linked to two of the aspects identified (**2 marks**) **or**
- **two** evaluative comments linked to **each of three different aspects** of the woman's meals (3 × 2 marks) **or**
- two evaluative comments each linked to two different aspects of the woman's meals (2 × 2 marks) **+ two further developed** evaluative comments **linked to two further aspects** of the woman's meals (2 marks).

Total: **6 marks**

Unit 2: Food Product Development

Chapter 5

Question 1

Cake A – has sunk in the middle
1. Cake has had insufficient cooking time.
2. Too much liquid has been added (to the mixture).
3. Cake has had too much raising agent added/been overbeaten.
4. Oven door has been opened during cooking.

Cake C – heavy, doughy texture
1. Not enough raising agent/plain flour used.
2. Out-of-date/damp raising agent has been used.
3. Not beaten enough.

Cake B – cherries have sunk to the bottom
1. Mixture too wet/too much liquid has been used.
2. Fruit wet/not dried.
3. Fruit not coated in flour.
4. Oven temperature too low.

3 × 1 mark; Total: **3 marks**

Question 2

Eggs	Sugar
1. Act as a raising agent/incorporate air. 2. Coagulation/helps set the structure/ framework. 3. Gives colour to the product. 4. Hydration of protein in the flour. 5. Adds nutritive value.	1. Sweetens/adds flavour to the product. 2. Makes the product darker/adds colour. 3. Incorporates air (when creamed with fat). 4. Shortens the mixture. 5. Increases shelf-life.

2 × 1 mark; Total: **2 marks**

Question 3

Change in proportion	Effect
Increase the proportion of flour in a sauce	The sauce will be thicker/more viscous. The sauce will gel.
Increase the proportion of sugar in a sponge	The sponge will be sweeter. The sponge will burn more readily. The sponge will sink in the middle. The sponge will be coarser grained. A sugary coating will form on the sponge. Any fruit will sink/collapse. The sponge will be darker in colour.
Increase the proportion of fat in pastry	Flavour will be richer. Pastry will be a darker colour. Pastry will be more fragile/crumbly. Pastry will be greasy.

3 × 1 marks; Total: **3 marks**

Question 4

Uses of fat
- Traps air when creamed with sugar, which helps baked goods to rise.
- Adds flavour and colour to baked goods depending on the fat chosen, e.g. butter.
- Provides shortness/crumbly texture to products such as pastry, cakes, biscuits.
- Increases the shelf-life/keeping qualities of sponges because they stay moist/soft for longer.
- Gives smoothness/gloss to sauces, which improves their texture and appearance.

2 × 1 mark

Uses of sugar
- Traps air when creamed with fat/eggs, which helps baked goods to rise.
- Traps air when whisked with eggs to give lightness/volume to the product.
- Helps bread to rise as sugar works with the yeast to produce CO_2.
- Adds colour when sugar caramelises on heating when making a syrup or during baking.
- Helps to preserve foods such as jam due to the high concentration of sugar.
- Gives correct texture to jams/confectionery due to crystallisation.

2 × 1 mark; Total: **4 marks**

Chapter 6

Question 1

Identify	Explain
1. (Correct) temperature/ warmth	5°C– 63°C is the danger zone – this is the best temperature range for bacterial growth. The best (optimum) temperature for growth is 37°C (body temperature). Food should be thoroughly cooked to a core temperature of 75°C or above to destroy bacteria. Food should be reheated to 82°C to destroy bacteria.
2. Food	Bacteria love high-risk foods – these are foods that: • are high in protein, e.g. fish, meat • can be eaten without further cooking, e.g. cooked meats • require refrigerated storage, e.g. poultry, dairy products, shellfish.
3. Time	Given the correct conditions, bacteria can divide in two every 10 minutes.
4. Moisture	Bacteria prefer a high water content to grow. When moisture has been added to dried food, then it must be treated as a high-risk food and stored correctly.
5. pH	Acidic/alkaline conditions help prevent food-poisoning bacteria multiplying. Bacteria will multiply at a neutral pH.
6. Oxygen	Aerobic bacteria require oxygen to grow. Anaerobic bacteria can grow without the presence of oxygen.

Identify: **2 × 1 mark**; Explanation: **2 × 1 mark**; Total: **4 marks**

Question 2
1. Food should be reheated thoroughly/till piping hot.
2. Food should reach a (core) temperature of 82°C.
3. Reheated food should be eaten immediately/should not be kept hot/warm.
4. Food should not be reheated more than once.

2 × 1 mark; Total: **2 marks**

Question 3
Raw meat and vegetables being prepared using the same knife

   i.

Potential hazard	Prevention
Transfer of bacteria from raw meat to vegetables. Cross-contamination of bacteria from raw meat to vegetables.	Use separate knife for meat and vegetables. Wash knives (thoroughly) in hot soapy water between preparing meat and vegetables. Use colour-coded knives.

Hot food being placed in the refrigerator to cool down

ii.

Potential hazard	Prevention
Temperature in fridge would increase, causing bacterial growth.	Leave food to cool (at room temperature for a time) before putting in fridge.
Increase in fridge temperature could cause other (perishable) foods to go off.	Keep fridge thermometer to ensure temperature is below 5°C.
Fridge temperature may not be low enough to stop moulds/yeasts forming.	Have separate fridge/blast chiller for cooling hot food in.

Each potential hazard: **2 × 1 mark**; Each prevention: **2 × 1 mark**; Total: **4 marks**

Question 4
Concept generation

1. Brainstorming ideas for a new product.
2. Development of ideas from market analysis.
3. Identifying a gap in the market.
4. To start the product development process.

Prototype production

1. Make a sample/specimen of the product.
2. To test the production line.
3. To test the product against the specification.
4. To find out the cost of a new product.
5. To allow modifications to be made before the product goes into full production.
6. To decide on the viability of the product.

2 × 1 mark; Total: **2 marks**

Question 5
Disassembly

1. To find out the components/ingredients of a competitor's product.
2. To find out the proportion of ingredients in a competitor's product.
3. To find out methods of manufacture of a competitor's product.
4. To find out about/compare similar products on the market.
5. To find out why a competitor's product is successful.

2 × 1 mark; Total: **2 marks**

Chapter 7

Question 1
Choice: Fruit smoothie B   **1 mark**

Sweetness – 3/satisfactory
1. Sweetness is 3/satisfactory so will be sweet enough for children/children will like it.
2. Sweetness is 3/satisfactory, so not too sweet so parents may be more likely to buy this for their children.
3. Sweetness is 3/satisfactory so we may promote this as healthy, encouraging sales.

Smell – 5/very good/very high
1. 5/excellent/best rating so will make it attractive to children/encourage children to buy.
2. 5/excellent/best rating so will encourage repeat sales.

Fruit flavour – 5/very good/very high
1. 5/excellent/best rating so children will enjoy it as most children like fruit.
2. 5/excellent/best rating so will encourage repeat sales.
3. 5/excellent/best rating, so parents may perceive this as healthy so may be more likely to buy.

Colour – 4/good/good
1. 4/good/second best rating will make it attractive to children/encourage children to buy.
2. 4/good/second best rating/may encourage parents to buy as it may not be too brightly coloured.

Consistency – 3/satisfactory
1. Consistency is 3/satisfactory so children will enjoy drinking the product.

3 × 1 mark; Total: **3 marks**

Question 2
Preference tests

1. These are used to supply information about peoples' likes and dislikes for a food product, e.g. 'smoothness'.

Rating test

1. Collects information/opinions about the specific attributes of a product.
2. Identifies specific strengths/weaknesses in a product.
3. Allows changes to be made to specific attributes based on the results.

Ranking/scoring/grading test

1. Used to find out how much someone likes or dislikes a product.
2. Helps manufacturer make judgements about the product in relation to one characteristic, for example flavour, texture, colour, etc.

Discrimination tests

1. To find out if the tasters can tell the difference between similar products.
2. To evaluate specific attributes, e.g. smoothness.
3. To find out if tasters can tell the difference if the proportions of ingredients are changed, e.g. if salt levels are reduced.

Paired comparison test

1. These tests help manufacturers test adaptations to their products.
2. To find out if tasters can tell the difference if the proportions of ingredients are changed, e.g. if salt levels are reduced.

Triangle test

1. To find out if consumers can identify the product on test from two other similar products.
2. To find out how similar/different the product on test is from the other two identical products.

Taste threshold test

1. Find out the minimum concentration of an ingredient before the product becomes unacceptable, e.g. reducing the amount of salt to an acceptable level.

Identify: **2 × 1 mark**; Explain: **2 × 1 mark**; Total: **4 marks**

Question 3

1. Helps manufacturer establish if there is a need for the product/gap in the market.
2. Helps manufacturer keep track of market trends.
3. Helps manufacturer find out what the consumer wants to buy.
4. Helps manufacturer establish where the consumer will buy the product.
5. Helps manufacturer establish the type of people who will buy the product/customer characteristics.
6. Helps manufacturer decide on the final price of the product.
7. Helps manufacturer establish how they are going to promote and advertise a product.
8. Enables manufacturers to gain public response as to how successful a product is going to be.
9. Allows manufacturer to monitor and evaluate a product's performance in the market place.
10. Competition from other manufacturers will be identified.

2 × 1 mark; Total: **2 marks**

Unit 3: Contemporary Food Issues

Chapter 8
Question 1
Religion

1. Consumers may not buy/eat foods because their religion states that it is forbidden.
2. In some religions there are particular foods that are eaten on special occasions.

Lifestyle

1. Consumers who have a higher income may choose to eat out/buy take-aways more.
2. Consumers who have a higher income may choose more 'luxury' foods.
3. Consumers who have a limited income may choose budget ranges of foods.
4. Consumers who do not have cooking skills may choose pre-prepared foods/meals.
5. Consumers who are health conscious may choose foods which follow GDA.
6. More consumers who snack/graze during the day may choose more snack-type foods.
7. Lifestyles may be busier, so more 'to go' option/ready meals may be chosen.

One answer from each: **2 marks**

Question 2

Facts	Opinion (linked to facts)	Consequence
Food items arranged in alphabetical order	Suitable Not suitable	1. He could find items easily/quickly. 2. He may be less likely to impulse-buy. 3. Similar items may not be grouped together and so could take time to find. 4. He may be more likely to forget items (if he is not using a list).
Weekly special offers available	Suitable Not suitable	1. The young single male will save money if he chooses these items. 2. These offers may encourage him to try something new. 3. May be more likely to impulse-buy/buy products which he does not need/overspend. 4. He may buy products which he cannot use before the shelf-life runs out/before they go off.
System remembers previous order	Suitable Not suitable	1. This may save him time when ordering. 2. He may be less likely to forget important items. 3. He may not save time because he will have to change the order if he wants different foods. 4. He may leave on items he does not need.
Substitute items sent automatically	Suitable Not suitable	1. He will not have items missing from his order. 2. He will not have to shop elsewhere to get them so it saves time. 3. The substitute item may be unsuitable/more expensive.
£5 delivery charge	Suitable Not suitable	1. He may consider the charge worth the saving in time/effort/petrol. 2. This will increase the cost of his (food) shopping.
Morning, afternoon or evening delivery slots	Suitable Not suitable	1. He works full time (and overtime) so will be likely to get a suitable slot. 2. He may not be able to wait in all morning/afternoon/evening for delivery.
Delivery available Monday to Saturday	Suitable Not suitable	1. He is likely to be able to arrange a suitable time. 2. He may not be able to arrange a suitable time as he is working.

Either:

- **four evaluative comments** each linked to different aspects of online shopping (4 × 1 marks) **or**
- **two evaluative comments** linked to **each of the two different aspects of** online shopping (2 × 2 marks) or
- **two evaluative comments each** linked to different aspects of online shopping (2 marks), plus **two evaluative comments** linked to a **third** aspect of online shopping (2 marks).

Total: **4 marks**

Question 3
Peer pressure

- Consumers may choose foods because their friends have them.
- Consumers may feel pressure put on them by friends to conform/choose particular foods.
- Consumers may choose/avoid particular items/foods/shops as they are/are not perceived as fashionable with peers.
- Consumers may choose different foods from their peers to demonstrate individuality.

One answer: **1 mark**

Shift patterns

- More mothers work, so may choose foods the children can prepare themselves.
- Shift work can result in families eating at different times of the day and as a result rely more on convenience foods.
- Workers can quickly microwave frozen or cook-chill meals when they come home or take them to work.

One answer: **1 mark**; Total: **2 marks**

Chapter 9

Question 1
Advantages

1. To protect food from damage/keep it in good condition (during transport/storage).
2. To keep food in a hygienic condition/protect the food from bacteria.
3. To prevent/show up tampering of the food.
4. To extend shelf-life of the food/keep the food fresh/in good condition.
5. So the food is presented in a convenient size/weight.
6. So the food is easily recognised.
7. To allow the food to be advertised.
8. To allow the food to be presented/displayed attractively (to attract the consumer).
9. To provide legal/useful information about the food.

Three answers: **3 × 1 mark**; Total: **3 marks**

Disadvantages

1. Can add to the cost of the food.
2. Some packaging is not environmentally friendly.
3. Can take up more storage space.
4. Can sometimes give the consumer a false impression of the contents.

One answer: **1 mark**

Question 2
Environmental issues

1. Consumer may choose vegetarian foods due to concerns over animal-related diseases or treatment of animals.
2. Consumers may be choosing natural/organic/unprocessed/additive-free foods because of concerns over manmade chemicals in foods.
3. Consumers may choose foods which can be cooked by microwave/induction hob/pressure cooker to save energy.
4. Consumers may choose foods in recycled/recyclable/no packaging to help the environment.
5. Consumers may choose cruelty-free/free range/dolphin-friendly/farm-assured food products because of concerns about animal welfare.
6. Consumers may choose foods which are produced locally to reduce the carbon footprint.
7. Increased interest in environmental issues has led to fewer genetically modified foods being produced/chosen.

Two answers: **2 × 1 mark**; Total: **2 marks**

Question 3

Fact	Opinion	Consequence
Random selection of fruits and vegetables which will vary weekly	Suitable Not suitable	1. The couple may enjoy planning meals round the contents of the box. 2. They may enjoy trying/cooking the variety of fruit and vegetables. 3. May not like the idea of not knowing what fruit and vegetables they will get. 4. They may not like some of the items sent. 5. They might not know how to prepare some of the items. 6. They may wish to buy specific/basic items which are not in the box.
Free delivery	Suitable/good	1. This will not increase the cost of their shopping. 2. This will save the couple the cost of fuel needed to go shopping.
Delivery Monday to Saturday 9.00am –6.00pm	Suitable Not suitable	1. One of them may be at home to take the delivery. 2. Although they both work full time, they may be more likely to be home on a Saturday. 3. Neither of them may be at home to take the delivery as they both work full time.
All produce grown within a 20-mile distance from customer	Suitable/good	1. It shows the couple that all items are grown locally/support local farmers. 2. It saves food miles, which might appeal to the couple.
Can order online	Suitable May not be suitable	1. They both work full time and they can order at a time convenient to them. 2. They cannot see the food before it is delivered/paid for.
Recycling symbol on cardboard box	Suitable Less suitable	1. The box is made from recycled materials which may appeal to the couple. 2. The packaging may increase the cost of the food. 3. The couple will have to dispose of the box.

Either:
- **four** evaluative comments **each** linked to a **different aspect** of the organic fruit and vegetable box (4 × 1 mark) **or**
- **two** evaluative comments linked to **each of two different aspects** (2 × 2 marks) of the organic fruit and vegetable box or
- **two** evaluative comments **each linked to a different aspect** of the organic fruit and vegetable box (2 × 1 mark) **plus two** evaluative comments **linked to a third aspect** of the organic fruit and vegetable box (2 × 2 marks).

Total: **4 marks**

Chapter 10

Question 1

Food additives

1. Some additives can cause side effects such as hyperactivity in children, so people with young children may avoid products containing additives.
2. Some additives can cause allergies so some people may wish to avoid products containing additives.
3. Some additives irritate sufferers of asthma and eczema so people suffering from these conditions may avoid foods containing additives.
4. Nutrients may be added to give the food qualities it did not have before so people may buy these foods to increase their/their children's nutrient intake.
5. Many new lower-fat products would not be available without the use of additives and people who are trying to lose weight may opt for these products.
6. Flavourings and colourings replace what has been lost in processing, e.g. green colour in peas, and people may prefer the foods containing additives because the colour is more like what they expect.
7. Consumers may avoid foods containing additives as they may be perceived as unhealthy.

1 mark

Functional foods

1. Functional foods could improve health and reduce the risks of certain diseases when taken as part of a balanced diet and healthy lifestyle.
2. Allow consumers to take greater control of their health through choosing functional foods for specific health benefits.
3. If there is a family history of heart disease, using a functional spreading fat/yoghurt/drink/omega-3 (which contains plant sterols) could help control cholesterol within the family.
4. Some foods, e.g. breakfast cereals and bread are a reasonably inexpensive source of additional minerals and vitamins in the diet.
5. Functional foods would have to be eaten in a fairly large quantity and for a long time to result in any improvement to health.

6. Functional foods can be quite expensive, which may prevent low-income consumers from being able to buy them.

2 × 1 mark; Total: **2 marks**

Question 2

1. A good source of protein instead of meat.
2. Is low in fat/contains no animal or saturated fats.
3. Provides vitamin B/zinc.
4. Convenient to use/no preparation needed.
5. The texture is not altered by freezing/cooking.
6. Does not shrink on cooking/is economical.
7. Low in calories/ideal for reducing weight.
8. Is a good source of fibre.
9. Readily absorbs flavours so can be used in a variety of dishes.

Two answers: **2 × 1 mark**; Total: **2 marks**

Question 3

1. Longer shelf life for perishable foods.
2. Consumers prefer the use of natural gases rather than preservatives.
3. Wider variety of foods available to the consumer all year round.
4. Food is enclosed in packaging which allows the product to be seen before purchase.
5. Packaging prevents food drying out/improves the storage of foods.
6. Product looks attractive as the colour does not deteriorate.
7. Better quality food has to be used for MAP.

Two answers: **2 × 1 mark**; Total: **2 marks**

Question 4

1. A wide variety of products is available so increases consumer choice.
2. Consumers who opt for 'healthy eating' products see chilled foods as 'fresh', less likely to contain additives and preservatives/better taste and quality.
3. Foods are usually easy to use, prepare, cook/reheat in a microwave and so can save time in a busy lifestyle.
4. There is a wide selection from which to choose, e.g. ethnic, vegetarian, so giving variety in the diet.
5. Cook-chill foods are produced in individual portion sizes and so are useful for people living on their own or on shift work.
6. There are a variety of price ranges, e.g. supermarket 'basic' or 'value' through to 'finest' ranges to suit different budgets.

7. Many cook-chill meals can be frozen at home so saves on shopping time and good for emergencies.
8. Someone with little or no cooking skills or who has difficulty preparing and cooking meals, e.g. the elderly can use them as they only require reheating.
9. Chilling does not affect food quality, colour, flavour, texture, nutritional value, making the product more acceptable to the consumer.
10. Can work out cheaper for people living on their own rather than buying individual ingredients to make the same dish.

Two answers: **2 × 1 mark**; Total: **2 marks**

Chapter 11

Question 1

Environmental Health Officer

1. To carry out a routine check.
2. To investigate a complaint from the public.
3. To enforce Acts/Regulations relating to food safety.
4. To inspect food to see if it is safe/take away suspect food to be tested.
5. To carry out a risk assessment.
6. To give advice.

2 × 1 mark

Trading Standards Officer

1. To carry out a routine check.
2. To investigate a complaint from the public.
3. To ensure all foods are sold in metric weights/measurements.
4. To ensure weighing/measuring equipment is accurate.
5. To ensure pre-packed foods are correctly weighed/labelled with the weight.
6. To check for counterfeit goods.
7. To enforce Acts/Regulations in respect of food labelling/to ensure food is labelled correctly.
8. To enforce the Trade Descriptions Act (1968).

2 × 1 mark; Total: **4 marks**

Question 2

1. Investigates complaints about food advertisements.
2. Monitors the accuracy of information given in food advertisements.
3. Monitoring for harmful or offensive advertisements.
4. Takes action against misleading, harmful or offensive advertisements, sales promotions and direct marketing of food products.

1 mark

Question 3

1. The CAB provides free, independent and confidential advice to everyone on their consumer rights and responsibilities.
2. If you have any food-related problems, Citizens Advice Bureau will give you advice on how to solve them.

1 mark

Question 4

1. Gives advice about the nutrient content of foods and dietary issues.
2. Helps people eat more healthily by providing information on healthy eating matters.
3. Helps to promote accurate and clear food labelling, so helps consumers make informed choices.
4. Improves food safety throughout the food chain, so reduces risks to consumers.
5. Agrees licensing of meat processing companies and regulates hygiene controls on meat and meat products.
6. Controls genetically modified food production.
7. Monitors the use of food additives.

2 × 1 mark; Total: **2 marks**

Chapter 12
Question 1

Information	Explanation
Ingredients list (in descending order)	The consumer can take account of likes/dislikes. The consumer can take account of allergies/intolerances. The consumer can take account of the proportion/amount of an ingredient in the product. The consumer can see if the product is suitable for a vegetarian.
Name of food	So the consumer is not misled/is clear about what is being bought. Names of certain foods are prescribed by law so the consumer is not misled.
Treatment/processing/conditioning of food	So the consumer knows of any process the food has undergone (accept appropriate examples, e.g. part-baked/dried/smoked).
Net quantity/weight/volume of product	So the consumer can compare prices. So the consumer can calculate value for money. So the consumer can check if the package contains enough for their needs/how many to buy.
Shelf-life: use by date	So the consumer can calculate the shelf-life of the food. So the consumer knows when the food will no longer be safe to eat/may cause food poisoning.
Shelf-life: best before date	Tells the consumer the date by which the food has best appearance/flavour/texture/nutritive value. So the consumer knows when the food will not be/taste as good but will still be safe to eat.
Storage instructions	So the consumer can store food to keep it in optimum condition. So the consumer can maximise the shelf-life of the food. So the consumer can enjoy the food at its best. So the consumer can check if they have the correct storage facilities.
Preparation/cooking instructions	So the consumer gets the best results/enjoys the product at its best. To ensure the product is safe to eat. So the consumer does not use the product wrongly (e.g. 'not suitable for microwaving').
Name and address/contact details of the manufacturer/packer/seller	So the consumer can contact the manufacturer in case of complaint/enquiry.
Place/country of origin	The consumer may wish to avoid products from a certain country. The consumer may wish to support a particular country (accept examples, e.g. produce of Scotland).
Lot/batch number	The consumer can identify any products which are recalled by the manufacturer.
Known allergens	The consumer is warned of potential health risk of specific allergens.

Identify: **3 × 1 mark**; Explain: **3 × 1 mark**; Total: **6 marks**

Question 2

a) Vegetarian Society
Consumers are reassured that:

1. Products with this label are free of animal flesh or any other product resulting from slaughter, e.g. meat or bone stock.
2. These products and ingredients have not been tested on animals.
3. The eggs must be free range.
4. Products must be GM free.
5. Products have not come in contact with any non-vegetarian products/ingredients during production.

2 × 1 mark

b) Soil Association
Consumers are reassured that:

1. The Soil Association's required standard for organic food has been met.
2. The foods have been grown without artificial fertilisers, which may be good for consumers with allergies.
3. They can select foods that have been made without man-made chemicals that may be harmful to health.

2 × 1 mark; Total: **4 marks**

Question 3

Product name

1. Important so the consumer knows what is being bought.
2. Important as consumer may identify with/have expectations of a particular brand.

Ingredients list

1. So the consumer can identify all the ingredients in the product.
2. Allows the consumer to avoid any ingredients they may wish to avoid/are allergic to.
3. May give the consumer an indication of value for money.
4. May help the consumer to judge the nutritional content/value of the product.
5. May help the consumer choose a low-fat/-sugar/-salt product.

Storage instructions

1. Allows the consumer to keep the product at its best before eating.
2. Allows the consumer to reduce bacterial growth/risk of food poisoning if the product is stored correctly.
3. The product can be kept in the best condition for a longer time/shelf-life so saving the consumer waste.

(Average) weight of product

1. Allows the consumer to compare prices/look for value for money.
2. Allows the consumer to calculate the number of portions in a product.
3. Allows the consumer to calculate how much to buy.

Use by

1. Allows the consumer to calculate the shelf-life of the food.
2. Lets the consumer know the shelf-life of the food before it becomes unsafe to eat.
3. So the consumer knows the date by which the food must be eaten if it is not to cause food poisoning.

Cooking instructions

1. Allows the consumer to cook the product so it is safe to eat/reduces the risk of food poisoning.
2. So the consumer can work out if they have the skills/equipment/facilities/time to make the product successfully.
3. Allows the consumer to cook the product successfully and enjoy it.

4 × 1 mark; Total: **4 marks**